'Enjoyed every second. Great dialogue, well-paced, very funny . . . Eddie's the down-and-out anti-hero we've come to love in British films, beginning with *Clockwork Orange*. Tortured, betrayed, hounded by enemies from all sides, he flashes and fumbles through a story that needs only a great soundtrack to become a cult classic.'
– *Triggerstreet.com* (review of screenplay)

'One Britpic well worth catching . . . this doggedly downbeat and defiantly droll hybrid of the psychological Western and latterday film noir marks Loftin as one to watch.' – *Empire*

OFFICIAL SELECTION
EDINBURGH
INTERNATIONAL
FILM FESTIVAL

NOMINATION
MICHAEL POWELL AWARD
BEST NEW BRITISH
FEATURE

'Startling UK thriller brings the grit of 70s Hollywood to a messed-up London estate . . . Sizzling with tension and vivid, near-surreal imagery, this is a forceful and confident debut' – Hannah McGill, Artistic Director, *Edinburgh International Film Festival*

'The likes of *Red Road* and *London to Brighton* have pumped new energy into the micro-budget sector, and *Saxon* deserves the same kind of platform. It's a refreshing surprise all round . . . definite cult potential.' – Michael Brooke, *Screenonline / Sight&Sound*

WINNER
SKILLSET EIFF
TRAILBLAZER

OFFICIAL SELECTION
BRITISH
FILM FESTIVAL
ISRAEL

'*Saxon* is a fast-paced, manga-styled sleuth movie – vibrantly colourful, rich with mordant humour, unapologetic in its cartoon violence, and slyly political . . . A literate, punk-inflected Western that strikes a savage vein of comedy.' – James Rice, Head of Screenings, *Edinburgh International Film Festival*

'All in, an impressive debut that reflects the years of effort Loftin spent honing the script before going into production.' – *The Herald*

'An off-kilter caper that emerges as one of the most refreshing crime films in years . . . the real star here is Loftin, whose surreal script is dark and downright hilarious' – *Metro*

'There aren't many occasions when you view a British movie and are struck by its uniqueness. Yet that's what happens when you watch Greg Loftin's directorial debut, *Saxon* . . . A triumphant micro-budget feature.' – *BBC Film Network*

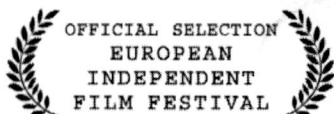

OFFICIAL SELECTION
EUROPEAN
INDEPENDENT
FILM FESTIVAL

WINNER
BEST EUROPEAN
DRAMATIC
FEATURE

'The opening twenty minutes has a brazen confidence as it swaggers into view like a combination of *Get Carter* and television series *Shameless*. The lively dialogue offers some amusing deadpan exchanges, the characters are intriguingly extreme and Sean Harris is an engaging, weasly underdog.' – *Screen International*

'A film that does for social housing what Woody Allen does for New York . . . one of the finds of the 2007 Edinburgh Film Festival.' – *Sneersnipe Film Review*

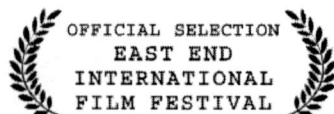

OFFICIAL SELECTION
EAST END
INTERNATIONAL
FILM FESTIVAL

NOMINATION
BEST UK DEBUT
FEATURE

'Sean Harris gets more impressive every time I see him . . . The treat for UK viewers is Matravers as the balefully aspirant Linda, prowling across the screen like a praying mantis in shiny stilettos . . . her casting is just too perfect for words.' – *Cinemattraction*

'Evoking the Leone style (wide angles and tight close ups) without slipping into parody, his action scenes are well paced and thrilling. *Saxon* is a confident debut and one of the funniest films screening this year.' – *Montage*

'It's a hugely assured piece of work by all concerned. Filmed on digital video, English council estates have never looked more luminously dire, and any film which starts with a man being chased by murderous fishmongers can't be all bad.' – *Cinemattraction*

'*Unforgiven* meets *Trainspotting*' – *Triggerstreet.com*

SAXON

screenplay by **Greg Loftin**

+ the making of a guerrilla film

CB *editions*

The DVD of this film, with interviews, behind-the-scenes footage and other extras, is available direct from www.peccadillopictures.com or from regular high-street shops and online stores.

First published in 2008
by CB editions
146 Percy Road London W12 9QL

Printed in England by Primary Colours, London W3 8DH

Screenplay by Greg Loftin
Introduction by Elise Valmorbida
© Sillwood Films Ltd

ISBN 978-0-9557285-4-9

www.saxonthefilm.com
www.cbeditions.com

Film distributed in the UK by Peccadillo Pictures Ltd
www.peccadillopictures.com

CONTENTS

INTRODUCTION:
The Making of a Guerrilla Film

Conventional wisdom and official statistics in 2005:
The average UK solo production film costs about £4.5 million to make. A guerrilla film is likely to cost £100,000 or less. Only 6 per cent of UK screens are dedicated to non-mainstream programming. As many as 95 per cent of all British feature films never get distributed (i.e. seen).

1999–2005

Starting with the seed of an idea, inspired by the people he met while making videos 'for the council' on derelict housing estates across London, inspired also by Greek tragedy (Oedipus and co.), Clint Eastwood's *Unforgiven* and *High Planes Drifter* and, yes, even *Chinatown*, Greg works on a screenplay called *Saxon*. There is revenge. There is violent redemption. There are bandages: across one character's nose, and across another character's eye.

Funding bodies reject his applications for funding. Apart from *Don Juan*, a surreal political short which premiered at the Santander Film Festival, and a Reading Independent Video Festival Award, Greg Loftin is an unknown. He's not connected. He's made lots of short films, but he's never made a feature before.

The script is pared down (fewer characters, fewer sets) to make the film dirt-cheap.

In 2002 Kevin Spacey launches Triggerstreet.com and the *Saxon* screenplay garners rave reviews.

2005

May Sillwood Films Ltd is incorporated as a Limited Company in the UK.

We take out a second mortgage, the maximum the bank will allow. The mortgage will be the funding base for *Saxon*.

We open a new Sillwood Films Ltd business bank account with Barclays, Soho Square. (Word has it that they know about the film business and how funny it is.)

We create a logo and style for Sillwood Films: rough, a bit punky, a bit Western.

sillwood films ltd ▪

June We send out letters to potential investors: 'You can buy as many shares as you like, but we're starting with investments of £500. We can't promise you a quick buck, but . . .'

In response, calls, envelopes and emails flood in. There are heart-warming good wishes, but there are also surprising silences. Some people back off. Other people offer time and support. And others invest what they can. Seven women over seventy invest much more than widows' mites. Neighbours dig deep. Old friends and new allies send money and love. Support comes from as close as next-door, as far as Utrecht, Detroit, Sydney and Melbourne.

Interviews by day and night, at home, in the office, in local bars and cafés. Production designers. Makeup designers. Costume designers. First assistant directors. Cinematographers. Everyone loves the script. Some people want more money than we have. Some people are wonderful but unavailable. Some are talented but precious. Some are keen but uninspiring. Some people are just right.

While keeping up with our day-jobs, we work into the small hours sorting through waist-high heaps of applications from actors and actors' agents, all promising to be The One. Shortlisting for auditions. Auditions. The world is heaving with quiz-show hosts and thugs, but we have trouble finding an Indian mother, Russell the bailiff, inexpressive twins.

Weekends are spent hunting out housing estates that satisfy the script's demands: dereliction, abandonment and, quite specifically, a large car-free concourse where a preposterous porch of Grecian grandeur can be built. There is a lot of bad housing in the world. We have both worked (in our day-jobs) for housing associations, and the good news for real people is that most social housing is being renewed. The bad news for *Saxon* is that most social housing is being renewed.

Reading and re-reading at every possible moment: *The Guerilla Film Maker's Handbook*. Lessons from case studies:

– The screenplay has to be brilliant. You can't make a good film out of a bad script.

– No matter how artistic the project is, get the legal rights right. You can't distribute a great film if your company doesn't technically own every single molecule of it.

– Don't be afraid to ask anyone and everyone for: advice, introductions, hardware, time, locations, services, skills, money, discounts, old flamenco tat. They may say no. But they might say yes.

– Get plenty of stills photographs during the shoot, and then some more.

– It's not a hobby. And it's not part-time.

July The director works with lead actors in a series of all-day rehearsals.

10 July All-day workshop in our kitchen. The director, producer, line producer, cinematographer, makeup designer, costume designer and production designer meet to get to know each other, interrogate the script, agree divisions of labour, discuss ways of saving money and/or time and/or lives. Initiates learn that a fake prop (e.g. weapon) is called 'a moody'. Fights, window-breaking and weapon-wielding all require unseen costly extras: safety pads, sugar-glass, fight coordinators, armourers. The makeup designer announces that she used to work with the daughter of real-life quiz-show host Henry Kelly. It could be a stroke of casting luck. The costume designer impresses us with his El Greco inspiration board – colours, light, drapery. And his line: 'No matter what resources you have, you go into every film saying we're making *Gone with the Wind*. You don't go in there saying this might get shown on cable TV some Monday afternoon.'

22 July First, speculative meeting with company lawyers Bolt-Burdon. Matthew Miller is our new ally.

24 July The cinematographer pulls out. (He has a small child. Another project has come up. It pays well. He's very sorry.) The shoot is scheduled to start in two weeks.

26 July First, speculative meeting with film/media lawyers Drew & Co. First lesson in shares, copyright assignments and star contracts. Andrew Curtis and Mark Johnson are our new allies.

27 July Heads of Department meeting in our kitchen – including the new cinematographer Steve Priovolos who must have been sent from heaven because he's talented, keen and, improbably, available. He even knows some of the crew already. Is he real? We are in awe/love.

6 August Location contracts negotiated, faxed, stamped, authorised, etc. Approval from the Tenants' Association. The Roundshaw Estate (once a set on *The Bill*) is going to be Saxon. It's already a ghost-town, as most of the tenants have left to make way for the bulldozers. The flats are beaten-up and boarded-up. There are 'free' design extras everywhere: unwanted furniture, household objects, graffiti of every colour and creed, a lavish choice of interiors. No need for costly sugar-glass: real windows can be smashed, as long as they are made safe afterwards. And there's a concourse to die for: a surreal car-free zone with plenty of space for Linda's and Kevin's provocative porch.

7 August We make up individual contracts for all cast and crew according to agreed fees, deferred fees and expenses. Computer drive explodes. There's even smoke. Line producer's car exploded earlier in the week. Will *Saxon* be like *The Exorcist*? There is an X in both names.

9 August First, speculative meeting with corporate accountants Derek Rothera & Co. Derek Rothera, Barbara Wills and Mehran Imanzadeh are our new allies.

8 August – 7 September THE SHOOT.

The next episodes in the story are told in a series of extracts from Newsletters to Investors, mailed out to everyone who had generously made possible what was taking place.

1 August 2005 All actors and crew are on board. Just as well – the production starts this Sunday! Shoot dates: 8 August to 7 September. Highlights on the people front include Sean Harris (*24 Hour Party People* et al) playing Fast Eddie, Sarah Matravers (*Footballers' Wives*) playing Linda, and Henry Kelly (*Going For Gold*, Classic FM) playing the quiz show host Nicko. Our makeup artist used to be a barrister and our award-winning cinematographer was a physicist. He's also Greek, which means that the Classical Greek elements in the script sing to his DNA. The crew is astounding: they are all hard-working and talented and in love with the script – they are certainly not doing it for the money. The line producer Sam Parsons is a whiz at everything.

If you bought 500 shares, it will pay for a runner for the entire shoot, or the total costume expenses budget or five actor-days. Great news for UK taxpayers: Sillwood Films Ltd ticks all the regulatory boxes for EIS, the Inland Revenue's scheme designed to encourage investment in high-risk enterprises . . .

18 August On Monday 15 August, the second camera assistant Jaime Goodbrand clapped his clapper for the 100th slate – an event which prompted ritual celebration from the crew. On the same day the same man did a nice bit of acting as a bailiff attacking a door with a battering ram. (We did warn you that the film contained violence, not to mention budgetary restraint.) And this

Saturday, another of our investors will be making a short appearance as a council tenant extra whose entire script is: 'No!' His will be one of the many vox pop voices comprising the chorus in this modern-day 'Greek' tragedy.

Speaking of Greeks, we are blessed with the most multi-ethnic crew you ever heard of. Greek, Turkish, Icelandic, Maltese, New Zealander, Indian, Chinese and African-Caribbean amongst others. And they all seem to be very brainy. The director is not short of ambient intelligence, even if he is short of sleep.

Ten days into the shoot, we have safely passed a few critical tests: no divas, no dramas other than the cinematic kind, no nasty surprises. This is of course not quite true. Every single day a new curved ball appears out of the blue: an actor has been double booked by absent agents, the rain changes its mind, a van breaks down, the sky is full of planes. But somehow pragmatism kicks in, schedules are reworked, contracts are rewritten, and the talent just gets on with it. This has been a week of hair and eyes: wefts, wiglets, cowgirl plaits, baldcaps, prosthetic eyelids, black eyes, eye-patches and prosthetic eyelessness.

2 September Today we issued Call Sheet 23. That means Day 23. Only 5 shooting days to go! Every day that passes, the risks diminish. The weather has been kind, we have clinched the last much-needed location (quiz-show champion Kevin's hideout), Eddie has sung his copyright-free Spanish ballad at Jackie's door, the windscreen of the bailiffs' van has been shattered and replaced without injury or litigation . . .

Since your last newsletter we've had good meetings with our newly appointed chartered accountants Derek Rothera & Co. Their job is to set up our accounts so that we are tax-efficient and all our investors are looked after in the best possible way.

On 1 September a 'dark horse' investor known as Otto celebrated his birthday and pledged to buy a lot of shares (the record number for any single investor after the dir/prod duo). This has earned him an end-roller credit as Executive Producer, alongside Barry Bassett of VMI who supplied top camera equipment and prime lenses at a price to please all investors . . .

7 September: 'The Miracle of Wallington'

Once upon a time there was a scribe called Gregory and for many years he wrote a wonderful story from his own imaginings. 'Lo!' he said, when his ink was dry at last. 'Let there be moving pictures for my story!' And his wife said, 'Moving pictures cost more than jewels or camels. Let us sell our goat and five chickens.' And other kindly people in the village gave them all manner of livestock and plenty. Even villagers seven seas away gave of their riches. And Gregory gathered about him a host of craftsmen and craftswomen to help him make the moving pictures. And so they travelled as one to the unholy town of Wallington, lying west of Croydon, where the houses were all falling down and the people wrote blasphemies on the walls. And every day Gregory battled against the plagues of low-costs, demons and things breaking. For weeks of days and weeks of nights he commanded the shape-shifters, the light-wielders and the weft-makers. And lo! He had his moving pictures in the can. And it was wrapped. And it was the seventh day of the ninth month. And people all about cried out in celebration at what they knew had been made. And from that day they knew it to be the Miracle of Wallington.

8 September Cast, crew, investors and partners escaped to the Costa Dorada for the wrap party. There was enough flamenco and sangria to create a happy ending for all kinds of characters, not just *Cielito Lindo* Eddie and España-loving Jackie.

Hangover? What hangover? The morning after the party, the irrepressible director began work on the rushes: transferring our stash of high definition tapes to standard definition tapes, using top equipment negotiated down in price by the producer who is now clinically deal-crazy. 30 tapes in all, each 50 minutes long, 545 slates. Or something like that.

September / October
- Apply to the Inland Revenue for EIS Scheme
- Digitise rushes
- Create moving sequence of stills on CD
- Design business cards
- Join NPA (New Producers Alliance)

- Accounts, accounts, accounts
- Contracts
- Seek funding for post-production
- Design and write marketing materials to create press-kit: production stills, synopses, talent, interviews, photo-book, press cuttings, 1-sheet . . .
- Design DVD cover for forthcoming teaser/trailer
- Attend training workshops at NPA

15 October Your *Saxon* producer had a very positive Business Breakfast on Thursday, pitching to industry execs, amongst them a financier, a sales agent and a distributor. They especially liked our slide-show, a dissolving sequence of stills from the shoot with music. All these people a) do not pull their punches, b) need to become Friends of *Saxon*, c) liked our pitch, d) want to see a trailer.

Not in our favour: the lottery that is this commercial competitive cautious business. The guerrilla filmmaker is an endangered species!

In our favour: the pitch, the screenplay, Henry Kelly's cameo as our quiz-show host, digital technology, our ability to finish. And, most of all, our lead: Sean Harris. Sean memorably played Joy Division's Ian Curtis in *24-Hour Party People*. He features in *Brothers of the Head* (a film about a New Wave band which premiered at the recent Toronto Film Festival) and *Asylum* (by *Young Adam* director David Mackenzie, with Ian McKellen and Natasha Richardson). It was after seeing Sean as Ian Curtis that we contacted him about *Saxon*. He loved the script and said yes. We auditioned nobody else. He *is* Eddie - a Londoner, a haunted young anti-hero, an Oedipal Clint! He gave us the performance of his life.

November Producer attends all-weekend Lo-to-no Budget Filmmaking course at the NPA to learn how to be, er, a producer.

Producer meets many people. Composers, music supervisors, sales agents, financiers, other producers. And Tim Adler, editor of *ScreenFinance*. And Mark Kebble, editor of *Angel* Magazine. New allies.

Surgery sessions with NPA's CEO David Castro – advice on trailer, on how to be a producer . . . Another ally.

Sillwood Films Ltd Share Issue No. 1.

23 November A positive meeting or two at the UK Film Council. They may have funds for our post-production. All we have to do is finish a rough assembly of the whole film, get a signed deal with an unofficially approved UK distributor, fill out a mountain of forms, and some months later, voilà. (The path of public funding never did run smooth.)

Speaking of rough assemblies, the director has reached the 30-minute moment, which is exactly one third of the final palaver. The rough assembly is made up of raw footage and raw sound. The music and sound effects are indicated but not finalised. Even the editing is raw. But it's enough to tell what kind of film is lurking in there. We're hoping for *Unforgiven* meets *Trainspotting*, as per the Triggerstreet review of the screenplay, the only difference being a few million dollars.

The director has also cut the trailer. This happened in stages. First, the three-minute version. Then the producer had a look. Then the two-and-a-half-minute version. Then the two-and-a-half-minute version with captions. The trailer is not a cinema trailer as such, more of a promo for the producer to show to potential buyers of the film: sales agents and distributors.

Trailer DVD sent out as a Christmas gift to investors.

WARNING: THIS TRAILER CONTAINS VIOLENCE, SOME BAD LANGUAGE AND INEXPRESSIVE TWINS.

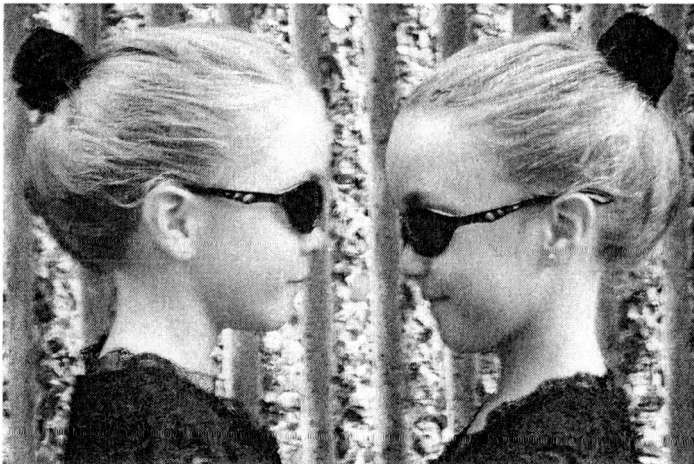

2006

1 February The editor has achieved a movie milestone: the rough assembly is complete. Yes folks, that's 100 per cent of everything in the right order (ish) and the happy assurance that there is enough footage to cover every scripted scene. Of course, the editing process must now continue, with countless polishings. Forthcoming adventures include sound design, ADR, grading and music, not to mention the icing on the cake: quiz show graphics and title design. Then after all the making, we must do another kind of making: a sale or two. Not a minor detail.

. . . which is why the director and the producer are heading for Cannes in May armed with whatever props we can handle: trailers, fliers, promo packs, possibly even a rough cut of the film. We are going lo-rent (Bed Bugs 'R' Us) and lo-cost (BYO baguettes). We're seeing the trip as a reconnaissance mission, ahead of the time when our film is actually ready to submit to festivals, so don't expect any great dramas, unless we are caught stealing food off a yacht.

Friday 3 February is National Music Day in *Saxon*. We sit with our two composers and watch the rough assembly from start to finish. The maestros have already begun 'noodling' (a musical term apparently). This is their first feature film gig, but they have done oodles of TV, not just noodles. They also have the backing of a renowned cinema composer who will act as our music supervisor. The labour is one of love rather than money. Your funds go far. We never say 'cheap' or 'free' when we mean 'deferred'.

8 March Michael Portman and Vincent Browett are confirmed as our composers and they've got past the noodling stage and into the full banana. They will be creating all the music you'll notice and all the music you won't. They are so talented they can do Johnny Cash, Bollywood, Flamenco and yes, even themselves! They make music out of spoons, sirens and Chinese State Radio crackles. *And* musical instruments too. There's not a note they can't handle. We love and depend on this kind of versatility. It's what *Saxon* is all about. Like everyone else in this fragilistic venture, the maestros are working on a deferred-fee basis.

It's not quite *Variety* or *Sight & Sound*, but *Angel* magazine is featuring our star Sean Harris in April after he agreed to do a rare interview and photo shoot. (Thanks to our lawyer-investors Bolt-Burdon for the lead.) This scoop will add a bit of gloss to our promo pack when we go to Cannes to steal food off a yacht.

25 April Latest news hot off the curling iron: we have a website. . . . As Frankie Avalon would say: surf's up! But now we really are showing my age. Thankfully the talented shares-for-web builder Michael Campbell is of a different generation – under 20 years old. Is it possible to be that young??

Other news. Music. Oh this is joy! Our two composers are getting more and more into the heart of the film and our latest session with them left us glowing with the heat of excitement. We have detailed musical sketches now for nearly all the tracks we'll need. There is 'literal' music (e.g. Rahim playing the radio) and the atmospheric stuff that is the soul of the film. This ranges from barely audible textures and soundscapes to arranged melodies. One track is called 'Saxon Breathing'. That's how subliminal it gets.

The composers will do anything and everything for their art. Chinese State Radio crackles? Ha. That's the least of it. Add Belgian cranes. Coat-hangers tied to the head, twanged and recorded through the bone. Breaking crockery played backwards. (!doowgdeW eht *toN*) At one stage Vincent had to leave the studio (he couldn't look), while Micky swallowed a miniature microphone wrapped in a plastic bag. 48V phantom powered. The maestros were after a soundscape which we had briefed as 'utterly subjective, internalised, muffled, shocked'. After this kind of instrumentation, Mexican trumpets start to sound rather conventional, although you won't say that when you hear them in context.

16 May Ascent Media Group – one of the world's top post-production houses – have offered to do the first stage of post-production for *Saxon* via their film facility St Anne's. The deal is this: we do post-production with St Anne's to a level that is film-festival-worthy. The image grading, colour work and visual effects will be of cinematic quality. The sound will be a good temporary dub – enough to feel cinematic without actually satisfying the full technical specifications needed for cinemas and distribution. If at that stage we go on to win a distributor (the next mountain to climb!) then we will come back to St Anne's for the final fee-paying stage. So loyalty is all, as it has been throughout the making of *Saxon*.

Your dir/prod team heads off to Cannes for a spell on 18 May. We have been advised to use this more as a low-key reconnaissance mission rather than a full-on sales trip because *Saxon* is not yet finished. The last thing we want to do is look like we're hawking shop-soiled goods at the next festival. So we are keeping a low profile, to match the low budget, quietly networking (and you know how quiet we are), and pointing the silent radar at English-language-film sales agents and distributors. We'll save the UK-based ones for meetings on our home turf, without the crush of the crowds/canapés. So we will be wearing sandwich boards saying: *desperately seeking sales agent! reliable distributor required! wealth & gsoh necessary!* Or something floaty/elegant like that.

5 July Cannes . . . Actually we stayed in La Bocca, which is down the coast a bit, in a very economical bedsit. We are still flushed with the excitement of the red steps and the rosé. We traipsed about the various sales salons and stands at the Marché, swapped business cards, stalked agents, left 1-sheets, pressed flesh. It was quite important for us to learn who's who and what's what. We did quite a lot of that. We are always learning, never earning. And no, we did not see Tom Hanks or his hairdo.

After Cannes, we got stuck into preparing *Saxon* for a test screener. Executive producer Barry Bassett of VMI generously offered us his 19-seat Soho cinema to use as and when we need it. Our first test screener happened on Friday 16 June. We had exactly 19 viewers who dutifully filled out feedback forms, contributed to a group discussion, and then talked some more in the pub afterwards. It was a terrifying but edifying experience for your dir/prod team. We had never before shown the film to such a gathering. And we had never seen the film so big, or with cinema speakers. Of course, the screener was the draft offline version, so the sound and image quality were extremely rrrrough. We moved quickly to create a new cut, still offline, still rrrough, but ready for a second screener on Friday 30 June. We have already re-edited since then, thanks to lots of helpful feedback from our audience. We hope to lock off this Friday and then there's plenty more post-production to do in partnership with Ascent from mid July. That's when the rrrough becomes smooth and lovely as Venus de Milo. (Was it a distributor who broke off her arms and legs?)

We know we can't please all of the people all of the time, but the feedback thus far has been generally very positive. We'd know by now if there was an elephant in the room; we've asked everyone to look very hard. Our audiences are a mix of investors, allies, and total parvenus. Young and old. Male and female. Our ratings are good, mostly very good, excellent. Most people say *Saxon* is original, gripping, involving, humorous, has a feel-good ending and great music. Only a few people thought the film was 'fair' or 'not my kind of film'. There were issues to do with pacing – we have fixed these now. Wherever possible, we have cut the uncertain bits, although nothing as serious as limbs.

15 September Post-production highlights:

TRANSFER TO HIGH DEFINITION – for those of us who were getting used to DVCam (the lo-res copy we've been using to edit) it was a joy to see the film in the lustrous, cinematic format we actually shot. *Think: cheap colour photocopy reverts to professional colour photograph.*

GRADING – a colourist patiently worked through scene by scene, enriching colours that were washed out by light or shadow, matching hues from one shot to the next within a scene, increasing light or shade for mood or clarity. *Think: lifting a veil off the professional colour photograph.*

TEMPORARY AUDIO DUB – a rich if temporary soundtrack which intensifies the action and travels all around you in a real cinema. The sound editor used our on-set recorded sound, created subtle audio layers where we needed to mask background noise or fill gaps, balanced the music and dialogue, boosted voices that were too soft, created certain effects (like audible motion through 3D space), and added sound effects to make you jump in your seat or wince or laugh.

RETOUCHING – our online editor began by comping in an aeroplane or two, darkening a few lit windows, and fitting the quiz show footage into a TV as part of the action. He continues very kindly to remove a few small but troublesome gremlins (copyright graphics we did/didn't notice, the shadow of a microphone, the edge of the camera barn-doors). This work should cost £700 per hour – and so it happens in down-time: lunch-hours, after-hours, gaps in the working day. We are in love with the team at Ascent / St Anne's and have offered to marry each and every one of them, in alphabetical order or order of appearance. Speaking of which . . .

END TITLES – yes, folks, that's where your name appears, sometimes more than once, because all of you invested, but some of you acted, designed, photographed, exec-produced and other jobs too many to mention here. (You'll just have to wait for the premiere and stay till the very end.)

17 November Sillwood Films Ltd Share Issue No. 2.

2007

1 January Post-prod work has been continuing, if not quite at the extreme pace of our youth. We have an interim copy of the film to show people, and we've started showing people. The process is slow. First, we have to woo them. Then we have to tempt them into coming along to our screening cinema. 'We're not famous,' we say. 'And we had a tiny budget, but we have something we think you'll really like.' Then, dammit, Christmas happens and the whole of London goes into a fog of hangovers and holidays. So the news is . . .

Sales agent 1 – watched the whole film. (The first thing we have learned is that nobody watches the whole film if it's rubbish. They would leave after 5–10 minutes. So, everyone tells us, watching the whole film is already a kind of reassurance.) But he doesn't like 'digital' especially in sunny daylight, although he feels it works better in the night scenes. Thinks Sean Harris is fantastic throughout.

Distributor #1 – watched a dvd. It's a good film but 'not right for us – we have to have a passion for it'. We sensed this company was a bit mainstream for us but we had a contact in common.

Distributor #2 – The Acquisitions Executive watched the whole film and 'loved it'. Found it to be 'funny and moving'. Said it had hints of *Shameless* 'which is a good thing!' Was genuinely very enthusiastic but had to 'go back to the office and discuss it with the others' before he could say too much. The others clearly had different ideas and the answer was no. They didn't have the resources to make it the success it deserved to be. He was very apologetic about being the bringer of bad news.

Distributor #3 – had a hangover. Three hours' sleep. Company's Christmas party last night. Watched the whole film. Said: 'It's a good film but we can only take on 3 or 4 films a year and need to put 5 months of work into each one.' Although his company released a film which is a cousin of *Saxon*, he said: 'That film was a very difficult decision to make. If we didn't have the press behind us, we would have had a hard time getting that to be financially successful at the cinemas. These days, you only get a week's slot, max.'

9 March We have today submitted the Corporate Accounts for the year ending 31 May 2006 . . . This is not quite the cheapest well-made feature film in history but it comes close. If we are to experience any more miracles, the one we really want is a distributor – to promote the film and sort out a cult following – whereupon those balance sheets might one day lose their brackets.

8 June

GOOD NEWS: *See No Evil* won the BAFTA for Best TV Drama. Our Sean Harris, who played the male lead role of Ian Brady, was up there on the BAFTA stage co-accepting the award. We are hoping some of this gold dust rubs off on our PR.

MORE GOOD NEWS: A respected film critic for *Sight & Sound* and Screenonline has viewed *Saxon*, first warning us that he would be 'brutally honest'. He was. He said there were a couple of negatives, but the list of positives was much longer. In fact, he wrote the most glowing review we could wish for. And he is going to translate his personal email into a publication-worthy review, attributed to him by name.

AMAZING NEWS: We have a UK distributor. (But don't get excited about money: our contract involves a tiny advance and costly hard work to come.) They are called Peccadillo Pictures and their emblem is a black cat, because they have one. They specialise in independent films: art-house (that's *Saxon*), gay and horror. Peccadillo are small but perfectly formed – and their star is rising. They've just got back from Cannes having signed the deal to distribute a film that went on to win the Festival de Cannes Critics' Week Award. And they have two films officially selected for the Edinburgh Film Festival. One is that same just-mentioned Cannes feature. The other is . . .

Saxon! Yes, dear Investor, *Saxon* has been officially selected for the 61st Edinburgh International Film Festival! This is the Holy Grail for us. The bee's knees. The total biscuit. Edinburgh is the best possible film festival in the UK. It's our 'Cannes'. It has a serious international reputation, a respected competition, a good PR machine, plus all the history and cred we need to prompt interest elsewhere.

Now all we have to do is *finish* the film! That means a not-temporary audio dub, some retouching, a tweak or two to the credits and voilà. All this (including the voilà) costs money – and we have sixpence in the bank – but we may have some room to manoeuvre now that we have a sprinkling of gold dust.

12 July Yesterday at midday the 61st Edinburgh International Film Festival relaunched the official website with all the details of this year's programme. We discovered a few marvellous things: *Saxon* will have its world premiere at 21.45 on 22 August and show again at 21.45 on Friday 24 August. Both screenings happen in the best cinema in town: The Filmhouse . . .

'Startling UK thriller brings the grit of 70s Hollywood to a messed-up London estate.' – The reviewer in this case is Hannah McGill, the EIFF artistic director herself. You'll read about 'Greg Loftin's forceful and confident debut' 'produced by Skillset/EIFF Trailblazer Elise Valmorbida'.

Today your dir/prod team attended the London Press Launch for the EIFF where your startled Trailblazer – one of ten 'hot new talents' in the UK – was lined up with a bunch of blokes for a photo shoot. Oh how we laughed. Is this all a joke? A trick? A dream? The artistic director actually named *Saxon* in her intro speech.

Then we picked up our goodie bag, fell out into the muggy sunshine of real London, opened the festival programme and discovered that *Saxon* is up for the Michael Powell Award for Best New British Feature. Then we really did fall over.

3 September At last a moment to write. Some notes from our festival diary . . .

Wednesday 22 August: 9 a.m. train from London King's Cross to Edinburgh Waverley
– Texts saying *Saxon* is in *Metro* newspaper: 4 out of 5 stars! More texts from strong contingent of EIFF-bound cast/crew + well-wishing investors worldwide
– 3 p.m. your prod joins panel of 'Women in Film + TV' (public admission of feeling like a fraud – is this a girl thing?)
– Festival Square: talismanic investor-actor-photographer Steve Mullins reveals that national broadsheet *The Glasgow Herald* has a feature on *Saxon* – more stars.
– Just then our *Saxon* trailer appears on the huge Festival Square public screen
– Hyped-up, wired + speeding BBC interviews of dir, prod + Sean at Filmhouse
– Festival Drinks followed by Festival Dinner followed by . . .

The World Premiere of *Saxon* at Filmhouse 1 (282 seats): a quick intro from the dir/prod team followed by a shocking onstage bouquet of flowers for our now-very-public 20th anniversary. Artistic director Hannah McGill watched the entire film again 'because I love it'. (We love Hannah.) Dear Investor, y/our film looked good. It sounded good. Cinematic. Was it the stars in our eyes? The audience laughed. In all the right places. Went quiet and scared in all the other right places. Clapped. No rotten tomatoes, no shoes, no dentures – although some people did leave. After a protracted onstage Q&A, cast, crew, investors, EIFF people and strangers sallied forth to the Cameo for drinks.

Thursday and Friday: Photocalls, interviews, meetings. Glimpsed a film or two. Chanced upon Saxonites. Gathered business cards. Fielded enquiries from other international film festivals. Found two BAD reviews. (Reality bites.) Attended the second screening of *Saxon* on Friday 24 August at Filmhouse 2. This time the cinema was cute and intimate (99 seats). More beloved Saxonites in attendance – thank you! More laughter. More applause. Then more drinking.

Saturday 25 August (the director's nth birthday): As we expected, no prizes for *Saxon*. But Nomination for the Michael Powell Award is prize enough. Not to mention the Trailblazer fandango. And our distribs picked up Best Director Prize for their film *XXY*. Good.

28 November It's three months since our heady-Eddie-Edinburgh days . . .

TABLOID NEWS: Sarah Matravers, *Saxon*'s female lead Linda, has been in the UK tabloids, after her soap-actor boyfriend's Celebrity Jungle entanglement with Catatonia's Cerys Matthews.

BAD NEWS: *Saxon* did not get into the British Independent Film Awards.

Some film festivals – and some cinemas – want only 35mm submissions. We can't afford a transfer to 35mm.

Two European sales agents have said no thanks.

Mr Acquisitions from a major TV brand said 'very original,

well photographed and well acted... a very good festival addition'
but no thanks for now.

Cairo Film Festival said no thanks.

GOOD NEWS: The British Film Festival in Israel said yes thanks.

A colossal UK distributor made us an offer we refused cos we
already had Peccadillo.

A North American sales agent said yes thanks, subject to
acceptance by Sundance. Forget bending spoons. All your powers
are required for Sundance or Slamdance.

Your dir/prod team were two on a Euroscript panel of three,
talking about *Saxon* — attended by 100 or so people.

We are working with Ravensbourne students to create a 1-minute
cinema trailer.

An excellent film production company is keen on Greg's next
script/s – *Saragossa* (a sort-of sequel to *Saxon*) and *The Hand
Factory* (another enclosed world with surreal and mythic under-
tones). This company has finance.

IMDb (Internet Movie Database) at last shows *Saxon* with a
star rating – after receiving a minimum number of online votes.
Our rating thus far is 8.9 out of 10. As Jackie would say of the
completed Eddie haircut: 'Not bad!'

The latest official review to be published is by David Perilli, a
journalist of *Rotten Tomatoes* and other filmic circles. New neat
quotelets: 'a film that does for social housing what Woody Allen
does for New York'; 'one of the finds of the 2007 Edinburgh Film
Festival'; 'Harris, a mesmerising character actor . . . fills the role
of Eddy with the weary naiveté of a character caught up in a
world running out of control.'

2008

20 February

Saxon was chosen from literally hundreds of new British films to feature in the British Film Festival in Israel (15th-26th January 2008). As an unexpected bonus, we were invited to attend the Festival as guests of the British Council. Your dir/prod duo was given a warm welcome by an impressive British Council team and a host of other cinephiles, including the founder of the Jerusalem Cinematheque Lia van Leer, Film Festival program director Avinoam Harpak, Cinematheque director Ilan de Vries – and Aviva Meirom, familiar to international audiences from the extraordinary feature documentary *Slim Peace*. While we were there, *Beaufort* was confirmed as an Oscar nominee for Best Foreign Film, so Israelis were generally feeling cinematic.

Saxon had three successful Cinematheque outings – in Haifa, Jerusalem and Tel Aviv – all with Hebrew subtitles. On the closing night of the Festival (just before *Brick Lane*) y/our film screened to a packed 370-seat auditorium. The Q&A sessions were upbeat. Despite its very British bent, *Saxon* seems to travel well.

Meanwhile, back at the rave. . . Our trailer competition at Ravensbourne College unearthed some talent and fresh perspectives, not to mention a lot of excitement. We've just awarded the first prize (a large jar of shiny pennies) to a pale sweet young boy-child whose depth of understanding and subtlety of editing defied the laws of everything. Your grateful prod has offered to marry him, but he'd certainly rather more cash.

We now have a new trailer for Peccadillo's other film DVDs so that the advertising of *Saxon* can begin. This trailer will be adapted to a 35mm format so that it can be shown at cinemas too . . . Speaking of 35mm, many film festivals and cinemas will only accept a 35mm print – which we can't afford. There is no official funding scheme in the UK for a 35mm blow-up, even though there is a fund for further copies once one has been made. £25,000 is all it takes. Any miracle-workers out there?

williamhill.co.uk (UK)
williamhill.ie (ROI)

0800 44 40 40 (UK)
1800 333 555 (ROI)

William HILL

Your bet is with William Hill Organization Ltd. and it is accepted in accordance with William Hill's Fair Deal Rules. We can be contacted on **08705 18 17 15 (UK)**, **00 44 8705 18 17 15 (ROI)** or via **customerhelp@williamhill.co.uk**

It's easy to bet...

Bet online at:
williamhill.co.uk (UK)
williamhill.ie (ROI)

Bet by phone:
0800 44 40 40 (UK)
1800 333 555 (ROI)

Your bet is with William Hill Organization Ltd. and it is accepted in accordance with William Hill's

10 March

Saxon has been officially selected for the European Independent Film Festival, known as 'Europe's Sundance'! With dramatic features from Poland, Kosovo, Hungary, Greece, Italy, Spain and the UK, the European Film Fest just happens to take place in the land of Lumière this year. Paris welcomes Gregoire Loftin with an exclusive directors-and-press-only boat cruise along the Seine. May the spirit of *L'Atalante* and *Les Amants du Pont Neuf* be with him! The Film Festival then proceeds to a press conference with skyscraping views of Paris and a weekend of intense screening activity at the Bibliothèque Nationale, from 14 to 16 March. *Saxon* is scheduled for its European outing, with French subtitles, on Saturday 15 March. Did you hear that? With French subtitles. Cute.

18 March: email to cast, crew & investors

We had to leave the European Independent Film Festival before the awards ceremony – second-last train home and all that. So we missed something very exciting.

SAXON WON THE AWARD FOR BEST EUROPEAN DRAMATIC FEATURE!

Can you believe it? We can't.

31 March

It feels like it's been a long time coming, but at last we are having a cast/crew/investor screening. With a difference. *Saxon* has been selected for the East End International Film Festival. This will be *Saxon*'s English premiere – in a brilliant indie cinema, with a general London audience. Plus your devoted dir/prod duo will be on stage for a Q&A, along with Michelle Connolly aka Jackie.

16 April: email to cast, crew & investors

The East End Film Festival screening of *Saxon* at 8.30 p.m. Monday 21 April is sold out. This is the first film in the whole festival to be sold out, and we are in one of the largest cinemas. There is a waiting list for returns. *Saxon* has been nominated for an award: Best UK Debut Feature.

8 December UK RELEASE OF *Saxon*.

PS – Have you heard the (true) story of the guy who traded up from one paper-clip to a house? The story of Saxon *is something like that. Only we paid for the original paper-clip with a house. Or something like that.*

SAXON THE SCREENPLAY

EXT: THE WOODS – DAY

EDDIE *is running for his life – three fishmongers in mucky whites are chasing him. EDDIE (white, late 20s) looks like a one-time punk. The woods come to an abrupt end – directly ahead is a high chain fence. We see EDDIE hit the fence with terrific force. He tries to climb but the fishmongers are on him.*

INT: WALK-IN FRIDGE, FISHMONGER'S SHOP – DAY

EDDIE *crouches in the corner surrounded by boxes of fish. He has a gag over his mouth and his hands are tied. He is wracked by violent shivering and barely conscious. SALMON is shouting at EDDIE. One of the fishmongers gets in behind EDDIE, grabs a good hank of hair and pulls his head back. SALMON is holding an oyster knife now, pacing up and down, his anger turning black. Then he moves in – stabs EDDIE in the eye.*

INT: HALL, PAROLE HOSTEL – DAY

EDDIE *is making a call on a public phone in a dingy hall. The phone is very damaged and the mouthpiece hangs by wires from the rest of the handset. The whole of this scene is shot in the reflection of a small dirty mirror above the phone. EDDIE has a great wad of grubby surgical dressing taped over his right eye. A drunk is singing somewhere out of shot.*

> EDDIE
>
> Hello Linda? It's Eddie . . . you remember – Eddie . . . Yeah . . . is Kevin about? It's just I need to borrow some money – ten – no ten grand – Linda?

Click – the line goes dead.

EXT: SAXON HOUSING ESTATE – DAY

We hear a deafening roar as an aircraft flies low over the roof of a block of flats – the undercarriage almost grazes the TV aerials.

We see an information board which gives a little map of the housing estate – it's old and heavily graffitied: 'SAXON HOUSING ESTATE, London Borough of Nobs'. EDDIE walks past in profile.

It's a sunny summer morning. We follow EDDIE as he enters the estate – a woeful sprawl of low-rise blocks with a single high-rise tower. Saxon looks abandoned – most of the flats are boarded up and blind.

EDDIE walks across an empty concourse. In the distance a figure leaves one of the blocks and begins to walk towards EDDIE. This is RAHIM (Bengali, early 20s) – he's dressed smartly in a shirt and tie. He has a large wad of surgical dressing taped across his nose.

Another aircraft is roaring low overhead. As the two men draw near, the tension mounts – the moment seems strangely fateful: two men with casualty faces. They pass each other and keep walking. Then, without slowing their pace, both simultaneously cast a rapid backward glance.

EXT: LINDA'S FLAT – DAY

EDDIE is scanning the names of the blocks and door numbers of the flats. EDDIE stops dead in his tracks. What is this? One of the ground floor flats is faced with white stucco and has an enormous Georgian portico stuck on the front. The portico is maybe twenty feet long with gleaming white columns. A red carpet leads to a shiny front door. EDDIE checks the address again, walks to the door and knocks. Pause. EDDIE knocks again. LINDA (white, mid 20s) calls through the closed door.

LINDA

What.

EDDIE

Linda?

LINDA

Who's that?

EDDIE

Eddie.

26

LINDA *opens the door. She is very pale, very pretty and dressed expensively in black. She wears a large gold cross on a chain around her neck.*

> LINDA
>
> Jesus – Eddie . . . You're wasting your time – I told you on the phone –

> EDDIE
>
> I was in the area – thought I'd say hello . . . Hello.

> LINDA
>
> What's wrong with your eye?

> EDDIE
>
> I got an insect in it . . . got infected – it's nothing.

LINDA *nods and controls a twitch of disgust.*
Pause.

> *(indicating the portico)*
>
> You're doing all right, ain't you – eh? . . . Greek, innit?

LINDA *casts a glance beyond* EDDIE *to see if they're being watched, then beckons him in.*

INT: LINDA'S FLAT, HALL – DAY

They stand in a cramped richly wallpapered hallway.

> LINDA
>
> Kevin's missing. Been gone two weeks.

> EDDIE
>
> Where is he?

> LINDA
>
> He's missing.

> EDDIE
>
> Did he leave any money?

> LINDA
>
> What!

EDDIE

That came out wrong – sorry.

CUT TO: DOUBLE OR QUITS – TV QUIZ SHOW

We see an extract of DOUBLE OR QUITS *on video playback. This is a cheap overlit quiz show, hosted by* NICKO *(white, male, 40s). There are three contestants, and in the spotlight at the moment and wearing a Hawaiian shirt is* KEVIN *(white, late 20s). He has a heavy forehead and a boxer's nose – the kind of face you rarely see on quiz shows.*

NICKO

So Kevin – which country was divided by the 38th parallel?

KEVIN

Korea.

NICKO

Correct – ten points. In what sport would you use a grinner?

KEVIN

Angling.

NICKO

Correct – are you by any chance a bit of an angler yourself, Kevin?

KEVIN

No – I'm a boxer.

Laughter and applause.
CUT TO:

INT: LINDA'S LIVING ROOM – DAY

LINDA *and* EDDIE *are watching* KEVIN *on playback on a huge plasma screen –* LINDA's *in a kind of trance. They're both smoking furiously.*

The living room is full of fancy goods, statuary, and dolls. Dominating the centre of the room is a huge chandelier.
CUTAWAY: DOUBLE OR QUITS:

> NICKO
>
> Which famous Beatles song featured a lethal tool?

> KEVIN
>
> Maxwell's Silver Hammer.

CUT BACK: LINDA'S LIVING ROOM
EDDIE *nods approvingly to* LINDA.

> EDDIE
>
> Yeah – he's good ...

> LINDA
>
> He overcame himself ... 'I'll double it, Nicko.'

She says this just ahead of:
CUTAWAY: DOUBLE OR QUITS

> KEVIN
>
> I'll double it, Nicko.

CUT BACK: LINDA'S LIVING ROOM

> LINDA
>
> Turned himself into a winner.

> EDDIE
>
> I got myself into a bit of trouble.

> LINDA
>
> He broke the record – scooped a million.

EDDIE

Yeah, I know.

LINDA
(pointed)
I know you know. I know that.

Pause.
CUTAWAY: DOUBLE OR QUITS

KEVIN

Artichoke.

NICKO

Correct – how many take part in a quadrille?

CUT BACK: LINDA'S LIVING ROOM

EDDIE

Must have a good memory ...

LINDA

Yeah he's got a good memory. Sounds easy doesn't it? But
you know what – we had to build his memory from scratch.

CUTAWAY: DOUBLE OR QUITS

NICKO

... a majestic deer?

KEVIN

Monarch of the Glen.

NICKO

Correct.

CUT BACK: LINDA'S LIVING ROOM
LINDA and EDDIE are in the corner of the room. This is Kevin's shrine
– photos of the champion boxer are flanked by fresh cut flowers. There
are shelves crammed with encyclopaedias, trivial knowledge books, etc.
LINDA nods towards the bookcase.

LINDA

He had to learn all them books – all of them. I was his coach
– I made him remember.

30

INT: LINDA'S LIVING ROOM – DAY

BEGIN FLASHBACK – the room is dark, Kevin sits on his boxer's stool wearing the full boxer's kit including a gum shield. Linda stands in front of him in the gloom.

                              LINDA
Come on – the fucking Cinque Ports!

Linda is wearing boxing gloves – she punches him.

INT: LINDA'S LIVING ROOM – DAY

                              LINDA
Took two years, Eddie – that's how you get a good memory.

BEGIN FLASHBACK as before.

                              LINDA
Who sang Dick-A-Dum-Dum?

                              KEVIN
Max Bygraves . . . ?

She punches him – a left and a right.
END FLASHBACK

INT: LINDA'S LIVING ROOM – DAY

                              LINDA
But you keep at it – 'cause the brain's a muscle, see – you work it, you make it fit.

BEGIN FLASHBACK
Now we see Linda massaging Kevin's head.

                              LINDA (VO)
I fed him special food, you know, brain food. And you know what, his brain got bigger, you could see it.

END FLASHBACK

INT: LINDA'S LIVING ROOM – DAY

>   LINDA
>
> Big – you know like a surgeon.

Linda's identical twin daughters enter the room. They're both dressed the same. They're eating cold roast potatoes.

> Oh you just help yourself now? Come over here – come on ... Iris, Poppy – this is Fast Eddie – we was at school together – say hello.

The twins, IRIS and POPPY (white, aged 6), are unnervingly inexpressive. They hiccup from time to time.

> Always gives them hiccups. (*To the twins*) Come on – mummy wants to talk to Eddie so you go and play in your room.

LINDA *leads the children out of the room.*

INT: LINDA'S LIVING ROOM – DAY

EDDIE *walks to TV.*
DOUBLE OR QUITS ON TV

>   NICKO
>
> ... hard luck to Laura but congratulations the money and the title goes to Kevin – very well done, Kevin.

EDDIE *picks up the TV remote and turns it off. He wanders around the room. He picks up an expensive-looking statue, turns it in his hand then hastily replaces it as* LINDA *returns. She sits and lights a cigarette.*

>   EDDIE
>
> When was the last time you saw him?

>   LINDA
>
> Two weeks ago.

>   EDDIE
>
> Where was he going?

>   LINDA
>
> Saxon Curry House.

                    EDDIE
Did he say anything?

                    LINDA
He said, 'I'm going for a curry.'

                    EDDIE
You reported him missing?

                    LINDA
                  (*irritated*)
What're you playing at?

                    EDDIE
I've been thinking – I could find him – you could pay me to
find Kevin. I could go out there and find him –

                    LINDA
Don't talk stupid.

                    EDDIE
I'm not – I've got local knowledge – this was my estate once.

                    LINDA
You just want the money.

*EDDIE seems ready to deny this but fails to find any words. He sits
wearily.*

                    EDDIE
So what do you think's happened to him?

                    LINDA
I don't know . . . I think . . .

                    EDDIE
What?

                    LINDA
I think . . . oh God . . . I think they might've killed him.

LINDA is crying.

                    EDDIE
Who?

                      33

> LINDA

The Council.

> EDDIE

Why would the Council want to kill Kevin.

> LINDA

'Cause of the porch.

EDDIE *chews on this information for a moment.*

> EDDIE

So what d'you think? Is it a deal?

LINDA *blows her nose.*

> LINDA

No.

EXT: SAXON – DAY

A slick black Mercedes drives at funereal speed around the estate.
LINDA is at the wheel.

INT: SAXON, MERCEDES – DAY

> EDDIE

Where's everyone gone, Linda?

> LINDA

A few changes since you been away.

> EDDIE

Is mum still here?

> LINDA

You don't know?

EDDIE *looks uncomfortable.*

Yeah she's still here ... you should go and see her ...

EDDIE *nods.*

Council done some dirty deal with the airport. Everyone's getting squeezed out. All this'll be knocked down for the new runway ...

> EDDIE

How come you're still here, then?

> LINDA

We ain't leaving.

> EDDIE

But you could live anywhere you like.

> LINDA

You don't get it, do you, Ed? You see, we're celebrities. We shine in people's lives –

As they turn a corner they see a small boy, hunkered down with his back to the car. LINDA slams on the brakes, sounds her horn.

> Oy – Oy! Move it!

ALI ignores her. He's playing with a dead bird. LINDA sighs and switches off the engine.

> What do you need the money for?

> EDDIE

I borrowed five hundred quid off this bloke called Salmon.

> LINDA

Five hundred's not a lot of money.

> EDDIE

Yeah – he lent it me before I went inside – now he's saying I owe him ten thousand.

> LINDA

Phew ... Do you have to pay him?

> EDDIE

He cut me eye out – says he'll have the other one if I don't pay up.

                          LINDA

I thought you said it was an insect . . . (*Pause*) All right –
maybe you can help . . .

                          EDDIE

I can find him, Linda.

                          LINDA

I want a professional job.

                          EDDIE

I need some money up front.

                          LINDA

Nah – slow down Eddie. No, I pay on results.

                          EDDIE

I'll start now.

EDDIE *gets out of the car – he hails* ALI.

What're you up to?

ALI *looks up.*

                          ALI

Do you want some lunch?

EXT: SAXON – DAY

VOX POPS
EDDIE *is conducting a door-to-door investigation – he knocks on
people's doors and stops them in the street.*

                          EDDIE

I'm looking for Kevin Potts.

                      TATTOO MAN

Kevin Potts – never heard of him.

                      WHITE WOMAN

What's up with your face?

                       WHITE MAN

No.

YOUNG MAN
Used to sign autographs – got on my tits.

YOUNG MOTHER
When he grows up he's going to be a boxer.

EXT: SAXON – DAY

EDDIE *stops an older woman in trainers and baseball cap. This is the* LIGHTERLADY *(white, 60s) – she is pushing a pram full of cigarette lighters.*

EDDIE
I'm looking for Kevin Potts – seen him about?

The LIGHTERLADY *looks surprised and suddenly upset – she pushes on and says nothing.*

EXT: SAXON ESTATE – DAY

VOX POPS

> WHITE MAN
>
> The council are telling us 'Get back in your box and shut the fuck up!'

> BENGALI MAN
>
> Double or Quits? No – Bengali people watch the other channel.

> WHITE WOMAN
>
> Wait there – I've got something for you . . .

She dips into her hallway. EDDIE waits. She seems to be talking on the phone behind the door. EDDIE turns and looks up at a clear blue sky. When he turns back the woman is holding a pepper spray and squirts it in his face. The effect is immediate: EDDIE drops to his knees, his eyes, nose and mouth stream, he can barely breathe.

> I've called the bailiffs – you're dead.

She slams the door. EDDIE is concentrating all his efforts on breathing.

EXT: SAXON – AFTERNOON

Now we see two figures heading towards EDDIE . They're bailiffs – they wear black boots and dark blue cargos, white T-shirts with 'The Bailiffs' emblazoned on the front, and the slogan 'Serving You Right!'

EDDIE gets to his feet and staggers away – he moves like a man unable to wake from a nightmare. The BAILIFFS are not far behind.

EXT: SAXON – AFTERNOON

EDDIE rounds a block of flats and gropes his way towards an open ground floor window where the curtains are drawn. EDDIE hesitates a moment then launches himself bodily through the window.

INT: SICK WOMAN'S FRONT ROOM – AFTERNOON

EDDIE lands on the bed of a SICK WOMAN (white, 70s). There is shock on both sides. The room is very dark.

SICK WOMAN

Arhhg!

Uproar. EDDIE is fumbling his way around the room – bumping into furniture, desperately trying to find a door out.

INT: LINDA'S FLAT, FRONT ROOM – AFTERNOON

EDDIE is sitting dabbing his good eye with a sponge. LINDA stands opposite, holding a glass of wine, giving EDDIE a 'I bought a dud' look. The TWINS sit quietly watching. EDDIE gets up, walks to the window and looks out at the porch.

EDDIE

Tell me about the porch.

LINDA

Council said we didn't have planning permission – so bailiffs come round and just destroyed it – smashed it up . . .
Course, when Kevin got home he – well he was annoyed – (*To the twins*) Daddy was a bit cross, wasn't he?

The TWINS stare back without expression. LINDA gets up and joins EDDIE by the window. She talks quietly so the twins can't hear.

He marched down to the Town Hall – hurt the Estate Manager quite badly – I ain't making excuses . . . I saw the photographs . . .

EDDIE

But the porch is still there.

LINDA

Yeah, well, that's Kevin . . . soon as he got home he put on another porch didn't he . . . big bloody idiot.

EDDIE

Look – I'm going to need somewhere to stay.

LINDA

Well you ain't staying here.

EXT: SAXON – DAY

MONTAGE SEQUENCE
We see the following:
– a young Muslim girl on roller blades
– several children gulping water from plastic bottles and fountaining each other
– a small kid catching a ride on the back of his grandmother's motorised wheelchair
– a plane taxiing

EXT: SAXON – AFTERNOON

EDDIE rounds a corner and walks past several public phones. One of the phones starts to ring. EDDIE slows, stops, turns back and lifts the receiver.

PHONE VOICE

(older woman's voice)

Are you the hero?

EDDIE

This is a phone box.

PHONE VOICE

You – are you the hero?

EDDIE is confused.

I can't sleep – I keep thinking about it – Please help.

Click. Line goes dead.

INT: LANDING OUTSIDE MRS PIERCE'S FLAT – DAY

The front door is painted hot pink – running all around the doorjamb are blinking fairy lights. The doorknocker is in the shape of a cat. The sound of really loud Country & Western music is coming from the flat.
   EDDIE knocks on the door. No reply. He tries again.

EDDIE

Hello? Hello mum, it's Eddie.

EXT: SAXON – DAY

The sun beats down – Saxon shimmers in a heat haze. EDDIE is walking in a furtive manner. He sees two BAILIFFS on patrol, he changes direction.

EDDIE's checking out the ground floor flats – most are boarded up, the doors sealed with sheets of steel. Now he stops outside a flat that hasn't been sealed. He looks through the window.

JACKIE

They've gone.

EDDIE turns. JACKIE is standing there (white, mid 20s) – an arresting young Irish woman with shaggy purple-streaked hair and thick eyeliner.

Who were you after?

EDDIE

I'm ... I'm looking for someone ...

JACKIE

I think you've got the wrong address – there's no one living there now. This is where the Quinns used to live. You know the Quinn family – you remember? It was all over the papers – terrible ... You've been out of the country or something?

EDDIE

Yeah.

JACKIE

Where?

                         EDDIE
What?

                         JACKIE
Where've you been?

                         EDDIE
Mexico.

                         JACKIE
What's your name?

                         EDDIE
Brad.

                         JACKIE
I'm Jackie. So Mexico – what's that like?

                         EDDIE
All right . . .

                         JACKIE
Do you cut your own hair?

EDDIE *looks sheepish.*

   I'm a hair stylist so naturally I'd notice . . . looks like a
   dog's arse.

INT: JACKIE'S FRONT ROOM – DAY

EDDIE *is about to have a haircut. He sits in a barber's chair – his
head sticks out of a sea-blue plastic tent. There's a washbasin and a
mirror in front of him and a large sign that reads 'Hair by Jackie'. The
room is a blend of the professional and the domestic. There's a big
Flamenco theme going on here: highly coloured posters of Flamenco
Dancers and moody Flamenco guitar music playing in the background.*
   *We see EDDIE's hair being washed, towelled dry, snip-snipped.
Details of gestures, friendly glances exchanged in the mirror.*

                         JACKIE
   . . . everyone knows they want to expand the airport.
   Council are set to make millions . . . over the ears?

EDDIE

Keep me sideburns.

JACKIE

Things've been really nasty here . . .

Pause.

EDDIE

What happened to that bloke – you know – Double or Quits? I heard he went missing.

JACKIE

Kevin Potts . . . I used to cut his hair you know . . . he came here quite a lot before he hit the jackpot.

EDDIE

He stopped coming?

JACKIE

Ah – he went funny.

EDDIE

What happened to him?

JACKIE *shrugs.*

What do you think?

JACKIE

Don't know – he went missing.

EDDIE

Where?

Pause.

Someone must know.

JACKIE

Who are you?

JACKIE *has stopped cutting his hair. She reaches across and turns the music off.*

I said who are you?

                    EDDIE
    I'm Eddie Pierce.

She looks blank for a moment – then suddenly anxious.

                    JACKIE
    I'm sorry, I can't cut your hair. Please go.

JACKIE *pulls the blue sheet off.* EDDIE *'s hair is only half cut and still
wet.*

                    EDDIE
    Yeah but you haven't finished –

                    JACKIE
    I want you to leave – I can't cut your hair!

EDDIE *makes no further protest. He heads out of the flat – a man
with a really extraordinary haircut.*

EXT: SAXON – DAY

VOX POPS

                    WHITE MAN
    Who cuts your hair – the council?

                 BENGALI WOMAN
                    (*vague* eyes)
    He's over there . . . He's looking at me . . .

                  BENGALI MAN
    He's a bloody racist.

EXT: SAXON CURRY HOUSE – DAY

*Saxon Curry House is a ground-floor flat with tables and chairs neatly
arranged in the front, and a dining space indoors. The ground floor
window is open – the sign above says 'Takeaway'. Amongst the tables
and chairs is a colourful abundance of flowers and shrubs in pots.*

    *There are no customers at this hour, only the owner and her family
sitting at one of the tables. MRS BEGUM (Bengali, 40s) is the mother,
and next to her is the youngest son ALI (seen earlier prodding a dead
bird). Her daughter is NADIMA (aka Dima, Bengali, aged 15), a sad*

and beautiful girl wearing a salwar and open-face veil – she sits peeling vegetables. The oldest son is RAHIM (the young man with the nose bandage seen near the beginning). RAHIM leans on the sill of the takeaway window scowling at the world while the rest of the family are chopping and peeling vegetables.

We hear the deafening roar of an aeroplane coming in to land. The atmosphere is very tense.

MRS BEGUM
Come and peel some vegetables.

RAHIM
I ain't doing that, yeah? – I ain't peeling – I'm wearing my good shirt.

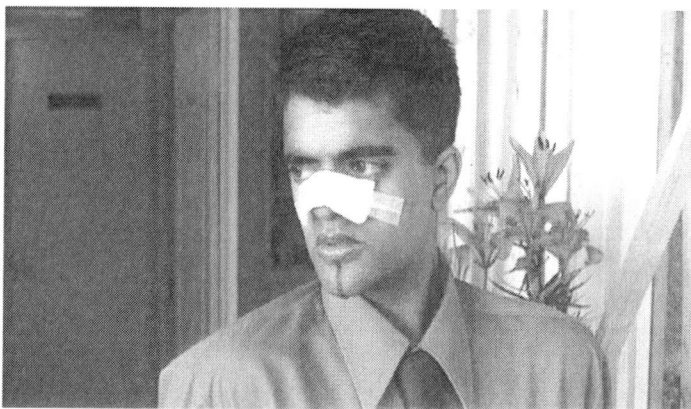

MRS BEGUM
Then you can do some shopping.

RAHIM
Send Dima.

MRS BEGUM
I'll get the list.

MRS BEGUM goes into the flat. RAHIM remains at the window scowling at his sister.

You take this and go.

MRS BEGUM *thrusts the shopping list at her son.* RAHIM *looks down at the crumpled paper in his hand – then strides over to his sister and drops it in* NADIMA's *lap.*

> RAHIM
> (*angry*)
> You – you go and do the shopping – the face, I'm tired of looking at it – get up!

MRS BEGUM *is hard on her son's heels.*

> MRS BEGUM
> Leave her alone!

MRS BEGUM *spins her son around and slaps his face hard. The dressing comes away and hangs from his cheek –* RAHIM *has a stitched and swollen nose. Mother and son are frozen for a moment.* NADIMA *is walking away fast.*

EXT: REAR OF THE EMPTY FLAT – DAY

We see a hammer striking a windowpane. EDDIE *pulls himself through the broken window and into the flat.*

EXT: SAXON – DAY

We see NADIMA *walking across the estate. She looks anxious; she keeps close to the buildings.*

EXT: EMPTY FLAT – DAY

EDDIE *opens the front door and kneels down to change the lock as* NADIMA *walks by. He watches – mesmerised. At that moment,* ALI *catches up with his sister and takes her hand. He casts a defiant look at* EDDIE.

EXT: SAXON – DAY

We see a figure pushing a panelled handcart. A sign on the side reads 'Molly's Seafood – cockles and mussels alive-alive-o'. Pushing the hand-cart is a strapping lad: MOLLY *(white, male, early 20s). He wears mucky white overalls and a yellow plastic trilby. His signature tune blares from a tinny tannoy:*

> *In Dublin's fair city where the girls are so pretty*
> *I first set my eyes on sweet Molly Malone*
> *As she wheeled her wheel barrow, through streets broad and narrow*
> *Singing cockles and mussels alive, alive-o.*

INT: EMPTY FLAT – DAY

EDDIE *turns a light switch on and off – no power. The flat is entirely empty.* EDDIE *hears Molly's signature tune getting louder and louder.*

Suddenly there is a loud knocking at the front door. EDDIE *peers down the hallway. Beyond the frosted glass of the front door stands a figure wearing a yellow hat.* EDDIE *waits. The letterbox clatters open and shut – a flyer is trapped in the flap.* EDDIE *creeps down the hall and gently removes it. We see it's an advert: 'Molly's Seafood – cockles and mussels alive alive-o'.*

EXT: SAXON CURRY HOUSE – EARLY EVENING

RAHIM *is taking an order from an old man with a red crepe face and a deep husky voice. This is* SNOUT *(white, 50s), and he's a bit drunk.*

SNOUT

Chicken Vindaloo ... saag bhaji, keema nan ...

EDDIE *is heading our way.* RAHIM *and* EDDIE *stare at each other for a few moments – they have seen each other before.* SNOUT *looks from one bandaged face to the other.*

Here – didn't I warn you lads about eating with chopsticks?

SNOUT *makes some short dry noises – this is laughter.*

'Ere, I know you.

EDDIE
(to Rahim)

I'm looking for Kevin Potts.

RAHIM

Yeah?

EDDIE

He's missing – you know where he is?

RAHIM

Is he missing?

RAHIM *looks blank.*

SNOUT

Oy – are you going to put my order in or what?

EDDIE

Who's the owner?

RAHIM

Look, man – d'you want to look at the menu or something – choose some nice food.

EDDIE

Is he in?

RAHIM

She's busy.

RAHIM *pushes a menu at* EDDIE, *who abruptly walks to the front door and tries to enter.* RAHIM *is already there.*

No chance – where you going?

EDDIE

I need to talk to her.

RAHIM

I don't think so.

They stand face to face.

EDDIE

What happened to your face?

RAHIM

What happened to *your* face? Huh? Someone poke you in the eye? So I'm telling you now, yeah, you got to leave.

EDDIE *moves in close to* RAHIM *and suddenly calls at the top of his voice.*

> EDDIE
>
> Service!

MRS BEGUM *appears behind his son holding a large kitchen knife loosely in her hand.*

> I'm looking for Kevin Potts.

> MRS BEGUM
>
> Who are you?

> EDDIE
>
> Private detective.

> RAHIM
>
> Oh yeah? Private detective now, yeah? That's nice. I think you better go – we got nothing to talk about.

> SNOUT
>
> Chicken vindaloo – hey, come on, Indian – you gonna put my order in, I'm starving.

EDDIE *looks from* RAHIM *to* MRS BEGUM *and then to* SNOUT. EDDIE *turns and walks away.*

> RAHIM
>
> You know him?

> SNOUT
>
> Oh yeah . . .

INT: HALLWAY OUTSIDE MRS PIERCE'S FLAT – DAY

EDDIE *is outside knocking at the door. The TV is blaring. No reply. Tries again. We see the letter box open –* EDDIE *peers inside.*

> EDDIE
>
> Mum? Mum it's me – Eddie. You in there?

No response. He pounds the door with his fists in frustration.

INT: THE SAXON TAVERN – EVENING

*Saxon Tavern is an utterly comfortless concrete bunker. There's a small
crowd of locals – all white. Two pot-bellied men are on bar stools –
both have pints in front of them as well as cigs, keys and loose change.
One of them is* PISSHEAD *(white, 40s), and the other* FRANKIE
(white, 40s – wears a brown hat, brown jacket and brown trousers).

PISSHEAD

. . . no you probably don't remember . . . they were big
bottles – they were called, what were they called . . . er . . .
big – like that . . . I can see them . . . they were . . .

FRANKIE

(*without interest*)

Quarts.

PISSHEAD

Quarts! Quarts – that's right, quarts . . . big bottles, like
that . . . held about two pints – not quite two pints, just a
little bit less than two pints – little bit less. Quarts. Nearly
two pints – little bit less...

SNOUT *sidles up to* FRANKIE.

SNOUT

'Ere.

PISSHEAD

Come and get us a drink, you old tosser.

SNOUT

Frankie.

FRANKIE

What?

SNOUT

Frankie.

FRANKIE

What?

50

SNOUT

Fast Eddie's back – Fast Eddie's back, mate. I seen him . . .

FRANKIE *struggles to get off his bar stool and falls over.* PISSHEAD *and* SNOUT *try to stand him up.*

PISSHEAD

It's all right – don't worry – don't worry – 'ere, come on, sit back on that stool and we'll have another pint eh?

FRANKIE *seems incapable of speech. He heads away – his legs moving jerkily like a stroke patient learning to walk.*

EXT: THE DUMP – EVENING

This is a tract of wasteland near the estate. It is strewn with every kind of domestic cast-off. EDDIE *is looking for something.*

EXT: SAXON – NIGHT

The estate is poorly lit at night. We see EDDIE *hauling a double mattress with some difficulty.*

EXT: SAXON – NIGHT

A woman in her sixties wearing a baseball cap and trainers is sitting next to a pram in which she has arranged a hundred novelty cigarette lighters. These lighters have bright flashing bulbs – the overall effect is a kind of miniature Las Vegas. The LIGHTERLADY *calls to* EDDIE.

LIGHTERLADY

They're two for a pound.

EDDIE *draws near – he nods and watches the twinkling lighters.*

EDDIE

All right – I'll have one.

LIGHTERLADY

Two for a pound. Two.

EDDIE

I only want one.

LIGHTERLADY *looks at him steadily. Pause.*

Go on then – I'll have two.

EDDIE *pays, takes the lighters and starts to move away.*

LIGHTERLADY

Put them away – hide them ... or they'll see you.

EDDIE *looks a bit spooked.*

EXT/INT: EMPTY FLAT – NIGHT

EDDIE *puts his key in the lock and enters, dragging the mattress behind him. He stops inside the black hallway – something is not quite right. In the dark, he props the mattress against the wall and silently edges down the hallway. He gently opens the door to the back room and enters.* BAILIFF #1 *slams the door behind him and turns on a powerful work light on a stand.* RUSSELL *(white, 30s) and* BAILIFF #2 *are standing in the middle of the room.* RUSSELL *is holding a clipboard.*

> RUSSELL
>
> Mr Pierce. Mr Edward Pierce. Estate business. Did you break that window Mr Pierce? *(pause)* That window – did you break it?

> EDDIE
>
> Russell.

> RUSSELL
>
> Did you break that window?

EDDIE *sighs.*

> EDDIE
>
> I'm squatting this place – that's my lock, these are my keys – yeah, I broke the window.

> RUSSELL
>
> Oh I see.

> EDDIE
>
> I don't want to take the piss but you're fucking trespassing.

All the BAILIFFS *stare at* EDDIE.

> RUSSELL
>
> Then we'll just have to obtain a court order to evict you.

RUSSELL *scribbles something at manic speed on a piece of paper, tears it off and pushes at* EDDIE.

> And here's the eviction notice.

EDDIE

All right – all right I'm going, yeah.

RUSSELL

I hear you've been doing door-to-door investigations. Am I correct?

EDDIE *glances towards the door – it's blocked.*

Did you obtain a licence? Would you like one? Would you like a Door-to-Door Investigator's Licence?

RUSSELL, *as before, scribbles something at manic speed, tears it off and pushes at* EDDIE – *it drops to the floor.*

Well, I'm sorry but the council's refused your application. Mr Flood – please seal the window up.

RUSSELL *moves to stand in front of the door.* BAILIFF #1 *and* BAILIFF #2 *position a sheet of hardboard over the broken window.* BAILIFF #2 *has a large yellow nail gun and very quickly works round the window securing the board in place. This is a noisy business.*

EDDIE

No, Russell, you – you don't have to do this . . . yeah? I mean what happened, . . . I just want to find Kevin Potts yeah?

RUSSELL *maintains a sour silence. The boys have finished boarding the window.*

I mean – oh fuck – where's Kevin?

RUSSELL

Well, Eddie, we had to take him to the Dump. That's where all the rubbish goes. (*pause*) Now I've got something else for you – this is from Barney.

RUSSELL *punches* EDDIE *full in the face.* EDDIE *hits the deck. Before he has a chance to recover,* BAILIFFS #1 *and* #2 *get stuck in.*

EDDIE

Fuck off!

RUSSELL

Fucking hold him.

54

                            EDDIE

    Fuck you!

                            BAILIFF #1

    Jumped up little tosspot.

EDDIE *is held down. Now* BAILIFF #2 *wraps* EDDIE's *jacket around his head.* RUSSELL *picks up the big yellow nail gun, walks over to* EDDIE *and kneels on his chest.*

                            RUSSELL

    You've got a fucking nerve coming back here –

EDDIE *is struggling maniacally – kicking in all directions.*

    You fucking murdering little fucker.

He starts to shoot nails into his arms.

EXT: A DITCH AT THE EDGE OF A MOTORWAY – NIGHT

The Bailiffs' panel van screeches away from the hard shoulder. EDDIE *has been thrown in a ditch. His right hand starts to probe the red mess of his left arm – his fingers lock on a nail head – he pulls out a one-inch nail. The traffic roars overhead.*

EXT: LINDA'S FLAT – NIGHT

LINDA *opens the door on a woeful-looking* EDDIE. *His arms are bleeding, his clothes are torn and bloody, his face is bruised – he is in pain and shivering.*

                            LINDA

    Eddie – my god –

EDDIE's *face suddenly screws up.*

    What is it?

EDDIE *sneezes twice.* LINDA *glances behind* EDDIE *left and right.*

    Get in.

INT: LINDA'S FLAT, FRONT ROOM – NIGHT

EDDIE *is sitting on a sofa in front of the big plasma screen watching Kevin and Linda's holiday video – sound of calypso music.* EDDIE *has his shirt off: his torso and upper arms are covered in bandages. The* TWINS *sit together on the sofa staring at* EDDIE. LINDA *enters.*

LINDA

Smoked salmon and asparagus all right?

EDDIE

Yeah.

LINDA

And there's a glass of wine there for you.

EDDIE

I don't drink anymore.

LINDA *gives* EDDIE *a tray of food. They watch the video.*

Looks like you're having a nice time.

LINDA

That was our first holiday in the Caribbean – been back twice . . . we love it . . . oh look, that's Freud – he was like our servant . . .

EDDIE

Is that your hotel?

LINDA

Five stars.

EDDIE

It's got a porch like your porch.

LINDA

You *are* a detective! First time I saw it I wanted it – that's mad, isn't it – to want a porch like that . . . anyway Kevin goes – 'Linda – if you want it – you can have it' . . . Bloody porch – wish I'd never seen it.

Pause.

Well Eddie, I'm going to have to let you go – you're crap at this, aren't you?

                    EDDIE
What?

                    LINDA
Look at you – first day on the job and you're all done in.

                    EDDIE
I'm just getting started –

                    LINDA
What happened to you?

                    EDDIE
I told you – the bailiffs were all –

                    LINDA
What happened to you?

                    EDDIE
Look Linda – I'm out there, I'm looking for him – I'm looking for Kevin.

                    LINDA
Yeah, but you're crap, Eddie.

                    EDDIE
I've got a lead.

                    LINDA
You've lost something Eddie. You're like a ghost.

                    EDDIE
                    (stands)
I'm sorry, Linda, but I happen to be in a lot of fucking pain!

                    LINDA
Excuse me!

                    POPPY
He said fuck.

EDDIE *starts to prowl up and down the room in a painful loping sort of way.*

> ### EDDIE
> Look – I better get back to work – Russell's given me a lead
> ... Yeah – I'm going to need a torch ... and a spade.

> ### LINDA
> A spade ...?

LINDA *looks frightened.*

> ### EDDIE
> It's just a lead ... I've got lots of leads – it's probably nothing.

> ### LINDA
> Oh Eddie ... a spade.

LINDA *is obviously distressed. She gathers her children and heads out of the room.*

> Come on – it's past bedtime ... come to bed little fish ...

EXT: SAXON – NIGHT

We see EDDIE heading through the empty estate carrying a spade. Now EDDIE is passing the public phones we saw earlier. One starts to ring. EDDIE answers.

> ### PHONE VOICE
> He's here – he's hiding in the dark.

> ### EDDIE
> Where!

> ### PHONE VOICE
> *(crying)*
> I'm frightened ... I can't sleep.

> ### EDDIE
> Give me a clue!

> ### PHONE VOICE
> Ask Tiny Fatima.

EDDIE

Tiny who?

Click. Line goes dead.

Hello? Hello.

EDDIE *slams the receiver down.*

EXT: THE DUMP – NIGHT

We see EDDIE, torch in hand, walking through the Dump. The torch beam darts back and forth across the rubbish-strewn ground. Now the torch lights up a high mound of cardboard and paper. He crouches and pulls away some paper – suddenly there is movement. The cardboard mound begins to erupt. EDDIE backs off rapidly. A TRAMP surfaces – drunk and deranged, he looks like a prophet.

THE TRAMP

It's happening again! It's happening again.

INT: LINDA'S FLAT, KITCHEN – NOON

This is an ostentatiously modern super-hygienic space. It is painted blizzard white and has so many fluorescent strips it hurts the eyes. LINDA is wearing a sexy silk dressing gown. She and EDDIE are drinking tea and smoking at the kitchen table. EDDIE looks bruised, dirty and tired. He has a fresh gash above the hairline – he dabs at it with a tissue.

EDDIE

Look, Linda, I was thinking ... maybe you're right – I'm crap at this.

LINDA

No, Eddie – no you're not crap. I just said that to get you motivated – and it worked – you went out and did some-thing. I'm a coach.

EDDIE

Awgh, Linda ... I've got to get away from here ... Russell and his fucking bailiffs are everywhere.

LINDA

No, Eddie, listen to me. You're feeling a little bit low now, you just need building up. I'll lend you one of Kevin's suits.

EDDIE

I don't want one of Kevin's suits.

LINDA pushes a finger to EDDIE's forehead.

LINDA

Eddie. Find Kevin. Look at me look at me – look at me. You go out there and you find Kevin. Wake up, Eddie!

She slaps his face. EDDIE gets off the stool and heads for the front door.

Don't leave me now, Ed – don't leave me! Don't – stop!.

EDDIE pauses.

I'll double it. I'll double it – twenty thousand. Twenty thousand, Ed. And look – look there's a thousand up front – see? – I was going to give it to you anyway. Go on you can count it – a thousand pounds, Eddie. Don't leave me now.

LINDA gives EDDIE a roll of notes. She suddenly hugs him.

Don't mind me, Ed – I'm just a little bit on edge ...

They hold each other for a moment. EDDIE breaks away and pushes a grubby finger under his eye-wad and scratches a serious itch in there.

You want to change that – looks disgusting ... Go and see Tiny.

EDDIE

Who?

LINDA

Tiny Fatima – the doctor.

EDDIE

Where is she?

LINDA

Wessex ... 'Ere – why don't you have a hot bath – make you
feel like a new man ...

EXT: SAXON UNDERGROUND CAR PARK – DAY

FRANKIE *is standing near a murdered car. He cuts a solitary figure in
his crumpled suit.*

FRANKIE
(*on his mobile*)
Yeah, I er ... I want to buy a gun. A gun, yeah (*Pause*) Well, it
doesn't matter – not important – wait – wait – wait – no,
don't go, listen – listen – I'm Frankie Hoogewerff –
Hoogewerff ... Yeah that's right – Barney –

FRANKIE *looks upset.*

He was my son ... my only boy ...

INT: LINDA'S BATHROOM/HALL – DAY

Fancy 'Roman' Bathroom. EDDIE *is sitting in a jacuzzi smoking. The
water is bubbling away.* LINDA *is in the hall outside the bathroom door.*

LINDA (OOV)
I've put out a nice suit for you, Eddie.

EDDIE
Kevin got any close mates anymore, Linda?

LINDA
He doesn't have many friends now to be honest ... things
are different when you're a celebrity ...

EDDIE
Family still about?

LINDA
His mum's still around – I think she's lost it though.

EDDIE
How d'you mean?

LINDA

Since Kevin went missing she runs away every time she sees me
... I don't know what's the matter with her ... she's fast too
— nearly seventy and she scampers around like a little rabbit.

INT: GUN DEALER'S FLAT, BEDROOM – DAY

*We see FRANKIE with the GUN DEALER (Cockney Sikh, 40s). They're
in a child's bedroom, the curtains are drawn. We see the GUN DEALER
removing his wares from a concealed drawer under a child's bed: all
kinds of knives, swords, sabres, catapults, crossbows.*

GUN DEALER

... I know what you're thinking — it all looks a bit more
traditional than you expected — am I right?

FRANKIE

I wanted a gun.

GUN DEALER

There aren't any — can't get hold of them for love nor
chocolate.

GUN DEALER *hands* FRANKIE *a bow.*

Go on — feel this.

*We see FRANKIE holding an African spear — looking miserable. We
see FRANKIE hefting a crossbow.*

What do you think — that's nice, isn't it? You could do a bit
of target practice — go on, I'll throw it in for you.

*The GUN DEALER throws some little paper fairground targets on the
bed.*

EXT: SAXON ESTATE – DAY

*We see a Bengali family being forcibly evicted from their flat — furni-
ture is being thrown out of the front door and window. An Asian airport
worker rubbernecks on his way home for lunch — he wears a peaked
cap, a day-glo yellow jacket, orange noise defenders and carries two
large table-tennis bats.*

EXT: SAXON – DAY

Molly's seafood handcart is parked in the middle of a concourse; a side panel is propped up revealing a beautiful still life of seafood on crushed ice. The sun beats down. MOLLY stands by himself listening to the flies.

INT: SAXON CURRY HOUSE, KITCHEN – DAY

NADIMA sits alone lost in her thoughts.

EXT: SAXON – DAY

EDDIE *is walking fast but furtively in his enormous suit. He passes the*
LIGHTERLADY *– she's selling her daytime goods: lighters in a galaxy*
of colours. She stares at EDDIE *as he walks past.*

EXT: SAXON – DAY

VOX POPS

WHITE MAN

Kevin Potts? – he ran off with my wife – only kidding.

WHITE WOMAN

I heard he was very rude to the Estate Manager.

TURKISH MAN
(*in Turkish*)

I don't approve of boxing.

EXT/INT: DR FATIMA'S HOUSE – DAY

We follow EDDIE *as he enters Wessex House. On a landing a free-*
standing board reads 'Dr Fatima's Surgery'. The front door is not locked;
EDDIE *passes through and straight into the living room. There are one*
or two patients waiting. A patient exits from the kitchen and EDDIE
walks straight in.

INT: DR FATIMA'S HOUSE, KITCHEN – DAY

In the kitchen, DR FATIMA *(African, 50s), a very tall woman, sits*
behind a table with the usual trappings of a GP. She has a filing
cabinet on wheels next to her. Directly behind are a washing machine
and a sink.

EDDIE

Tiny Fatima?

DR FATIMA

Doctor Fatima.

EDDIE

I'm not well.

64

DR FATIMA

Neither am I – you have to wait outside.

EDDIE

It's my eye.

DR FATIMA *advances towards* EDDIE.

DR FATIMA

You'll have to wait. Please.

EDDIE *suddenly slams the kitchen door shut, and leans against it.*

Are you drunk?

EDDIE

No.

DR FATIMA

I know you.

EDDIE *looks blank.* DR FATIMA *walks to the sink and washes her hands.*

A few years ago I was called to your mum's place – you were there . . . and there was another man, a bailiff – he was dead . . .

EDDIE *looks troubled.*

You don't remember me?

EDDIE

No.

DR FATIMA

You were drunk.

EDDIE

I don't drink. I stopped.

DR FATIMA *nods* EDDIE *to a chair. She moves across and peels back the surgical tape – the dressing comes away. She screws her face up to examine* EDDIE's *eye. She makes some unhappy clucking sounds.*

DR FATIMA

What's happened here?

65

                              EDDIE

My eye's itchy.

                            DR FATIMA

You should go to A&E straight away . . . it looks quite evil.

DR FATIMA *sets to work swabbing the eye with disinfectant. Now she
applies a much smaller dressing.*

                              EDDIE

I'm looking for Kevin Potts.

                            DR FATIMA

I know.

EDDIE *looks surprised.*

      Keep still . . . The whole estate knows . . .

                              EDDIE

I was told that you – you might know where he is.

                            DR FATIMA

You were misinformed.

                              EDDIE

She said –

                            DR FATIMA

She was wrong.

DR FATIMA *has dressed* EDDIE's *eye – now she slips on a black eye
patch. She comes around and talks to* EDDIE *face to face.*

      You and your friend Kevin Potts are a disease on this estate.
      Get out.

EXT: SAXON – DAY

We see EDDIE *wearing a new black eye patch walking furtively in
the shadows. He notices another lone figure walking very fast in a
different direction. This is the* LIGHTERLADY *– she has a large rucksack slung over her shoulder. Their eyes meet.* EDDIE *watches her till
she's out of sight.*

EXT: JACKIE'S FLAT – DAY

On Jackie's front door is a big brightly painted sign: 'Hair by Jackie'. There are fashion photos of beautifully coiffed models all around the door. EDDIE knocks. JACKIE opens the door.

EDDIE

Any chance of finishing my hair?

JACKIE abruptly closes the door.

JACKIE

Go away – I'm not cutting your hair.

They talk either side of the door. EDDIE takes out the wad of cash Linda gave him and pushes a fifty-pound note through the letterbox.

Jesus – what's this?

EDDIE

Where's Kevin?

JACKIE

Take it back – I'm not touching it – would you stop bothering me!

She pushes the money under the door.

EDDIE

Yeah but Jackie – you used to cut his hair . . . you gotta know something. Jackie?

INT: COMMUNAL STAIRS – EVENING

A SICK OLD WOMAN is heading up the stairs, sweeping the steps with an enormous broom as EDDIE is heading down.

SICK OLD WOMAN

I know you, don't I?

EDDIE

Do you?

SICK OLD WOMAN

You're Irma's boy.

                    EDDIE

No – sorry.

                SICK OLD WOMAN

Got your mother's looks – she had a funny eye . . .

                    EDDIE

I'm looking for Kevin Potts.

                SICK OLD WOMAN

He's missing.

                    EDDIE

I know.

                SICK OLD WOMAN

Ask the Lighterlady – she knows everything that goes on at
Saxon.

                    EDDIE

The Lighterlady.

                SICK OLD WOMAN

Lives over at Mercia. You can't miss her – she's the only one
left in the whole building now. I think she's got a telescope.

EXT: SAXON – NIGHT

One bored kid lights and flicks matches at another smaller kid.

EXT: SAXON – NIGHT

*We see EDDIE moving towards Mercia House. Some way off, across
the concourse, EDDIE notices the Seafood handcart – Molly is
nowhere to be seen. EDDIE moves on, closing the gap with Mercia
House – a great dark tombstone of a building. High up, on the
twentieth floor, at the very top of the building, a single light shines in
a window. Someone is looking out.*

                    MRS PIERCE

Hello darlin' – all on your own tonight?

EDDIE's *gaze is suddenly brought back to earth – MRS PIERCE (white mid 50s) lurches towards EDDIE. She has a sot's face buried deep in make-up. EDDIE keeps walking.*

Come on, spring sale – everything must go.

MRS PIERCE *laughs.* EDDIE *keeps walking.*

Blow job for a fiver – come on, big boy, what d'you say?

EDDIE *stops and turns.* MRS PIERCE *is drunk. She looks at* EDDIE *very closely now; her face twitches through a range of emotions. Then she slaps his face hard.*

Where have you been? Where have you been!

MRS PIERCE *begins to cry – she fumbles around in her handbag for a tissue – she looks destroyed.*

(pulling herself together)
Have you eaten, Eddie?

                    EDDIE
Yeah.

                  MRS PIERCE
So ...

                    EDDIE
Well, I knocked on your door but no one answered.

                  MRS PIERCE
Oh, was that you? Are you a pirate now then, Eddie? I didn't recognise you ...

                    EDDIE
I was going to come round and see you later.

                  MRS PIERCE
I know ... come tomorrow, not tonight – I'm busy tonight.

She abruptly walks away – a bit unsteady on her pins.

EXT: SAXON – NIGHT

The TRAMP walks by himself – in his hand he holds a dead bird.

                  THE TRAMP
It's happening again – it's happening again!

EXT: MERCIA HOUSE – NIGHT

EDDIE *arrives at the foyer of Mercia House.*

INT: MERCIA HOUSE, LIFT – NIGHT

EDDIE *enters the lift. A recorded voice in the lift says 'doors closing – going up'. Perhaps it's because the message is running slow, but this sounds like the voice of the saddest woman in the world. Every floor is announced: 'second floor, third floor ...' On the twentieth floor,* EDDIE *steps out of the lift.*

INT: MERCIA HOUSE, LANDING – NIGHT

As soon as the doors close we hear the sound of the lift travelling back down. This puzzles EDDIE. He turns and finds the flat where he thinks the LIGHTERLADY lives. He knocks on the door.

                              EDDIE
    Hello?

He knocks again.

    Hello? Look, you don't have to open the door – I just want
    to talk. Is anyone there?

He knocks again.

    I'm looking for Kevin Potts.

There is a sound from behind the door.

    He's an old schoolfriend of mine – someone said you
    might've seen him.

Silence. EDDIE knocks again. He turns his good eye to the lift count-down. The lift has gone all the way to the ground floor.

    You can talk to me . . . I bought two lighters off you yester-
    day . . . man with the mattress – remember me?

EDDIE waits a few moments longer, then walks back to the lift and presses the button. Nothing. EDDIE presses the button again. Nothing. EDDIE is puzzled.

INT: MERCIA HOUSE – NIGHT

EDDIE *sets off down the stairs. After he has made some progress, he hears a noise – someone coming up?* EDDIE *stops – silence. He carries on a little further – sounds like footsteps. He stops again – silence. He starts to climb down the stairs again – very, very quietly. He turns onto another landing – the way ahead is clear. Then* MOLLY *steps into view.*

> MOLLY
>
> Something wrong with the lift. What do you think? Probably broken down . . .

EDDIE *notices something gleaming in* MOLLY's *hand.*

> Oh this? This is an oyster knife, Eddie –

EDDIE *blinks and immediately turns and runs back up the stairs.* MOLLY *very soon catches up and wrestles him to the ground. He holds the oyster knife close to* EDDIE's *face.*

> Don't fuck about, don't fuck about. Come on, then. Where's the money? Where's the money? Salmon's money. Hey! Salmon's money!

MOLLY *kicks* EDDIE *in the head. He stops struggling.*

> EDDIE
>
> I'll have it tomorrow.

> MOLLY
>
> What am I supposed to do with that? I'm looking at you man, and all I see is like a pile of shit on the landing. And you're telling me you'll have the money tomorrow – are you fucking sure?

MOLLY *starts stamping on* EDDIE.

> EDDIE
>
> Whoa – arghh – I'm doing a job for Linda Potts!

> MOLLY
>
> Loads of quim, yeah? Real fucky-fucky-fucky-fucky-fucky-fucky –

EDDIE

She's paying me!

MOLLY *pulls back.*

MOLLY

Okay, Eddie. That's okay. I was just kidding . . .

MOLLY *casually goes through EDDIE's pockets and removes his wad of cash.*

I knew you was doing that gig. Good money eh? – nice suit. Yeah . . . You've got till tomorrow Eddie . . . or I'll stab you in the eye.

MOLLY *turns and rapidly heads downstairs. EDDIE has a gash on his forehead.*

EXT: SAXON – NIGHT

EDDIE *walks across a very dark estate – a plane roars close overhead.*

EXT: JACKIE'S FLAT, LANDING – NIGHT

EDDIE *is knocking at her door. JACKIE opens the door a fraction on a security chain.*

JACKIE

Jesus – what? What's the matter with you – why d'you keep bothering me? Leave me alone.

JACKIE *swiftly closes the door.*
    EDDIE *opens his mouth to speak. Then, miraculously, he starts to sing a Spanish ballad – hesitant at first, but tender, and sounding surprisingly good.*
    On her side of the door JACKIE is astonished.
    EDDIE *breaks off and says a few words in Spanish.*

EDDIE
(*in bad Spanish*)
Please help me – I have big problems . . .

She opens the door on the chain again and stares at him.

73

EDDIE bursts into song full volume. JACKIE lets him in quickly.

INT: JACKIE'S FLAT, FRONT ROOM – LATER

We hear Flamenco music in the background. EDDIE sits in the barber's chair and dabs at his new wound. JACKIE is sitting in an armchair still holding the kitchen knife.

JACKIE

You can finish up then go. So how did you get a face like a pizza?

EDDIE

Help me.

JACKIE

I don't know anything.

EDDIE sits back in his chair. Pause.

Well ... okay – it's not a lead but it's ... I don't know what it is ... (*pause*) When Kevin won all that money he went completely off his head. You heard what he did at the Town Hall. (*pause*) Anyway he came around here this one time ... he was all excited – waving money around ... I don't know how he got it into his head but he thought he could just come in and – buy me. I was very scared ... he ... I told him to get lost ... he hit me ...

JACKIE is crying.

He ... said he was sorry – he wanted to give me the money ... I didn't take it ... that's not true ... I took the money ... (*pause*) I don't feel good about it. I'm saving to get away from here – that's the only reason.

JACKIE blows her nose.

EDDIE

I could help you.

JACKIE

Be quiet.

74

EDDIE
Jackie – do you want to put the knife away?

JACKIE
No, I don't – you're a murderer.

EDDIE *gets up and walks to the door.*

Where're you going? Finish your tea.

EDDIE *turns.*

EDDIE
It was manslaughter – not murder.

INT: LINDA'S FLAT, FRONT ROOM – NIGHT

LINDA *stands alone, a glass in one hand and a cig in the other, gazing into her fabulous chandelier. She lets her hand play across the glass jewels. Now her eye is drawn to a movement beyond the front window. For the briefest moment we see a face there – RAHIM – then it's gone. LINDA looks frightened – she runs to the window and closes the curtains.*

INT: SAXON CURRY HOUSE, LANDING – NIGHT

NADIMA *sits on the landing.* ALI *joins her and places a drawing in front of her.* NADIMA *stares at the picture. Ali talks excitedly about the picture – he's trying to cheer her up.* NADIMA *seems to be a long way away.*

INT: JACKIE'S FLAT, FRONT ROOM – NIGHT

EDDIE *and* JACKIE *sit opposite each other.*

> EDDIE
>
> ... they'd smashed her flat up – her face was a bloody mess ... Barney'd broke her nose, cheekbone ... couple of teeth ... she put up a fight – Barney was just standing there laughing at her ... don't remember much after that. I was drinking a lot back then.

> JACKIE
>
> I never believed she'd steal a wallet off a bailiff – I remember reading it in the papers and I thought she'd never do a thing like that ...

> EDDIE
>
> She took his wallet ...

> JACKIE
>
> You should leave Saxon.

> EDDIE
>
> Can't.

> JACKIE
>
> How much is Linda paying you?

EDDIE *isn't saying.*

> Are you a bounty hunter? Clint Eastwood, is it? Get out of Saxon. You're no good at this sort of work – will you take a look in the mirror.

> EDDIE
>
> I've got to finish the job.

Pause.

> I'm in trouble – yeah? I've always been in trouble . . . trouble leads to trouble that's what they say – trouble leads to trouble which leads to this trouble which leads to that trouble and that trouble looks like the same fucking trouble all over again . . . But it's all going to change. It has to. When I find Kevin I'm going to go to Spain. I'm ready. See?

EDDIE *whips out his passport and shows* JACKIE – *it obviously means a lot to him.*

> Live in the sunshine . . . swim in the sea . . .

EDDIE *gets up and starts singing his Spanish ballad again.*

JACKIE
Arrgh – pack it in . . . I said stop it!

EDDIE
Do you know what prison taught me? Spanish. When I was a little boy, my mum had this Spanish boyfriend . . . he was a lot smaller than her – tiny little head . . . Called himself Jesus . . . he left a big impression on me . . .

JACKIE
What happened to him?

EDDIE *shrugs.*

EDDIE
He went back to Saragossa – but I've still got his address . . . Saragossa – sun sea and Eddie. You heard the one about the Spanish fireman? He had two sons – one called José . . . the other called Hose B.

JACKIE *smiles indulgently.*

> Could I stay here tonight. On the sofa.

JACKIE
Now you're telling jokes.

EDDIE
I'll pay you.

EDDIE *pulls out a fifty pound note.* JACKIE *is put out.*

>   JACKIE
>
> Go to your mum's.

>   EDDIE
>
> She's – busy.

>   JACKIE
>
> What about Linda's?

>   EDDIE
>
> She's mad.

JACKIE *looks uncertain.*

>   JACKIE
>   (*cold*)
>
> All right – give it to me.

She stands and takes the money.

EXT: SAXON – NIGHT

Full moon. The twins POPPY *and* IRIS *are walking around the estate by themselves in their nightdresses.*

EXT: SAXON – MORNING

We see airline stairs – twenty feet high – being driven across the estate.

INT: JACKIE'S FLAT – MORNING

JACKIE *brings* EDDIE *some tea – he's sitting up, wide awake.*

>   JACKIE
>
> Did you sleep?

>   EDDIE
>
> No – don't really sleep much . . .

JACKIE *smiles as she grabs a hank of* EDDIE's *hair.*

>   JACKIE
>
> Maybe you just need a decent haircut.

INT: JACKIE'S FLAT – LATER

JACKIE *has finished cutting* EDDIE's *hair – she pulls off the sheet.*

>   JACKIE
> Let's look at you – not bad. Come on and have something
> to eat.

>   EDDIE
> No – better get going.

>   JACKE
> Then take this.

JACKIE *is holding out the fifty-pound note.*

>   EDDIE
> What?

>   JACKIE
> Take it back – you're not a bad person … take it – it's too
> much anyway.

JACKIE *tries to give him the money.*

>   EDDIE
> I don't want it – you could use it to get away from here.
> Could go to Spain.

>   JACKIE
> You're out of your head.

EDDIE *heads for the door.*

>   EDDIE
> I'll come back for you when this is over.

>   JACKIE
> Get lost.

>   EDDIE
> I like you.

>   JACKIE
> Hey Eddie – do yourself a favour – get on the bus. Go
> home.

EDDIE *and* JACKIE *hold each other's eyes silently for a moment.*

Take care.

EDDIE *walks out into the bright sunshine.*

EXT: SAXON – MORNING

EDDIE *walks across a wide empty concourse. Now he becomes aware of the faint sound of a phone ringing.* EDDIE *looks about him – in the distance we see the public phones.* EDDIE *runs and lifts the handset.*

> PHONE VOICE
> What are you doing?!

> EDDIE
> What?

> PHONE VOICE
> You're no good – you're not the hero! You said you'd find him – you're not trying – I can't sleep –

> EDDIE
> But you're not helping me, are you?

> PHONE VOICE
> I can't believe he did that – I keep thinking about it . . .

EDDIE *is scanning the estate. He sees a figure far in the distance – the* LIGHTERLADY. *She is standing next to her pram wearing her signature baseball cap and trainers – she's holding a mobile phone.*

> EDDIE
> It's you – look just –

She's running – surprisingly fast for a woman her age.
EDDIE *gives chase – he jumps over the wall and heads towards her. She dips into a block of flats.*

INT: BLOCK OF FLATS – DAY

EDDIE *follows the* LIGHTERLADY *into the flats – he runs up the stairs and along the open walkways. He's lost her.*

EDDIE *is done in — he staggers out of the building and leans against a wall to get his breath back. He is breathing hard and looks quite ill.*

EDDIE *now becomes aware of a strange buzzing sound. A small boy wanders across the wide empty concourse. Closer now we can see this is* ALI *— he is whirling a bullroarer on a piece of string. He is wearing a little sandwich board: on the front is written 'lunch special today — Chicken Korma' and on the back 'Saxon Curry House'.* ALI *sees* EDDIE *and walks over to him still whirling his bullroarer — the noise is weird and unsettling. They stare at each other for a few moments —* EDDIE's *face is shiny with sweat. He falls over in a dead faint.*

We see ALI *running away. Blink. Then we see him returning.* EDDIE *is lying on the ground where he fell.*

ALI

Hey — mister. Hey. Are you dying?

EDDIE

No.

ALI

Have you got AIDS?

EDDIE

What's your name?

ALI

Ali.

EDDIE *is sitting up now — he rubs his head where he hit the ground.*

Are you hungry?

EDDIE *grunts.*

Come and have some lunch.

EDDIE *isn't moving.*

My brother wants to see you.

EDDIE

Who's your brother?

Rahim.

EDDIE

Why not.

EDDIE gets slowly to his feet. They begin to walk off together.

ALI

Are you still looking for that boxer?

EDDIE

Who says I'm looking for anyone?

ALI

Everyone knows you're looking for him.

EDDIE

Do you know where he is?

> My brother chased him away.

                    EDDIE

> Why?

                    ALI

> 'Cause he wrote his name in Dima's book. And Rahim got
> angry and the boxer punched him in the nose.

                    EDDIE

> Who's Dima?

                    ALI

> My sister.

EDDIE *lights a cigarette.*

> You shouldn't smoke – Are you going to shoot him?

                    EDDIE

> Why would I do that?

                    ALI

> Rahim says you kill people.

                    EDDIE

> No, I don't do that.

EXT: SAXON CURRY HOUSE – DAY

*We see ALI and EDDIE arrive. RAHIM is drying glasses and setting
the tables. RAHIM nods EDDIE to enter.*

INT: SAXON CURRY HOUSE, FRONT ROOM – DAY

*RAHIM ushers EDDIE to the empty dining space in the front room.
EDDIE sits at a table.*

                    RAHIM

> Saxon Special?

EDDIE *nods.* RAHIM *heads for the kitchen where* MRS BEGUM *is
preparing food.*

INT: SAXON CURRY HOUSE, KITCHEN – DAY

RAHIM *tears off his order and impales it on a board.*

> RAHIM
>
> One Special.

> MRS BEGUM
>
> What's he doing back here?

RAHIM *is heading back out.*

> Rahim! I want him to leave right now!

> RAHIM
>
> Customers waiting.

INT – SAXON CURRY HOUSE, FRONT ROOM – DAY

RAHIM *sits down opposite* EDDIE.

> RAHIM
>
> Nice suit – bit large.

> EDDIE
>
> What do you want?

> RAHIM
>
> I'm looking for the boxer. So are you.

> EDDIE
>
> Did he break your nose?

Pause. RAHIM *leans forward.*

> RAHIM
> (*whispers*)
> He did my sister. Yeah, that's right . . . She's fifteen . . .

> EDDIE
>
> I'm sorry . . .

> RAHIM
>
> I don't want you to be sorry – I don't even want you to talk about it. Don't talk about my sister. (*pause*) So, I'm saying – you and me – we find the boxer.

EDDIE

You don't know me.

RAHIM

I know you killed a bailiff.

EDDIE

You don't know anything about it.

RAHIM

Vengeance, man – I know what it is.

EDDIE

I was drunk – I didn't mean to kill no one – I don't even
remember doing it.

RAHIM

What're you saying?

EDDIE

I'm saying – I was drunk and I don't remember.

RAHIM

Man – they must've brainwashed you or something cause I
know you took a hammer to that bloke's head and you killed
him dead.

EDDIE

You're not listening me –

RAHIM

You're pretending like –

EDDIE

Now I'm telling you – I was drunk – mad fucking brain-dead
drunk – and I don't remember nothing. You got that?

MRS BEGUM *arrives at the table with a huge plate of food.*

MRS BEGUM

You eat this then you leave.

RAHIM

It's okay – this isn't Fast Eddie – this is just a small man in a
big suit.

EDDIE
(*To Mrs Begum*)

It's okay – I'm going.

RAHIM
(*whispers*)

Wait, wait, wait –

Behind EDDIE, *through the window, we see two* BAILIFFS *making their way across the concourse towards the restaurant.*

(*whispers*)
Bailiffs coming, man – go through the back – now.

BAILIFF #1 *is looking straight into the room as he draws closer.* EDDIE *gets up and heads out of the room.* BAILIFF #1 *sticks his big head through the open window.*

BAILIFF #1

Hey, Raymondo.

RAHIM

Yo – Lol.

BAILIFF #1

Whose is that, then?

RAHIM

You staying for lunch? Check our menu, we're doing your favourite today – we also got a low carb curry special –

INT: SAXON CURRY HOUSE, HALLWAY – DAY

EDDIE *is in the hallway surrounded by closed doors.*

INT: SAXON CURRY HOUSE, FRONT ROOM – DAY

RAHIM
– coz I know you're watching your weight.

BAILIFF #1

Whose dinner?

                    RAHIM

What.

                  MRS BEGUM

   I'll set up a table.

BAILIFF #1 *nods towards* EDDIE's *plate.*

                  BAILIFF #1

   Whose dinner is that?

                    RAHIM

   Just like a guy who came in – yeah ... He coming back
   though – after.

                  BAILIFF #1

   Don't move.

Suddenly, BAILIFF #1 *disappears from the window,* BAILIFF #2
remains outside. Now BAILIFF #1 *strides into the front room – he
walks up close to* RAHIM.

   Put your hands in the air.

                    RAHIM

   Woah, man – what's up with you?

                  MRS BEGUM

   I think there's been some mistake –

                  BAILIFF #1

   Stay out of it, Mrs Begum – hands up.

BAILIFF #1 *claps his hands and holds them together in the shape of a
gun. He points the 'barrel' at* RAHIM.

   One move and you're dead.

                  BAILIFF #2

   He's a nutter.

Now he snatches two onion bhajis from EDDIE's *plate and stuffs them
into his mouth.*

                    BAILIFF #1
                    (*mouth full*)

Bhaji Burglar!

                    BAILIFF #2

Hoo! Hoo!

                    BAILIFF #1

Bhaji Burglar!

                    BAILIFF #2

Hoo! Hoo!

                    BAILIFF #1

Bhaji Burglar!

BAILIFF #1 *runs around triumphantly punching the air.*

INT: SAXON CURRY HOUSE, BEDROOM – DAY

EDDIE *has tried a couple of doors – both are locked. The third gives –
he enters a bedroom.* NADIMA *sits on a bed, her back to the door,
staring at the wall.*

                    EDDIE

'Scuse me –

NADIMA *turns – her startled response swiftly shades to terror.*

– how do I get out of here?

NADIMA *is beside herself – she gives an ear-splitting scream.*

INT: SAXON CURRY HOUSE, BEDROOM – DAY

NADIMA *is crouching in the corner – she can't stop screaming – the*
BAILIFFS *run in –* EDDIE *has escaped through the back window.*

EXT: SAXON – DAY

EDDIE *is racing across the estate. The hunt is on –* EDDIE *staying
just ahead of the* BAILIFFS. *Eventually* EDDIE *dips into a rubbish
alcove and squeezes behind a large panekin. The* BAILIFFS *run past.*

A moment later we hear a violent explosion of noise – the panekin rocks – someone two storeys up has thrown a hundred bottles down the rubbish chute. EDDIE calms down and tries to make himself comfortable. He falls asleep.

Now we hear someone approaching. EDDIE wakes with a start. The LIGHTERLADY walks by carrying a rucksack.

EDDIE follows her around several blocks. At one moment the LIGHTERLADY looks over her shoulder – did she see him? She doesn't change speed or direction.

INT: BLOCK OF FLATS, BOILER ROOM – AFTERNOON

The LIGHTERLADY enters a block and goes down to the basement then on to a boiler room. She opens a small metal door and ducks inside. EDDIE listens at the metal door a few moments then enters. Ahead of him is the opening to an inspection well. EDDIE peers in. The LIGHTERLADY is holding a torch and climbing down the metal rungs. EDDIE ducks out of sight and waits for her to clear the well.

INT: INSPECTION WELL – AFTERNOON

EDDIE makes it down to the bottom of the well. He holds one of his disco lighters aloft. A tunnel leads away. EDDIE removes his shoes, ties the laces together and slings them around his neck. He sets off down the tunnel.

EXT: SAXON – AFTERNOON

In the distance we see four BAILIFFS walking towards us – at the head of the group is RUSSELL. They're carrying axes, crowbars and sledgehammers. They look like big trouble.

EXT: SAXON CURRY HOUSE – AFTERNOON

RUSSELL and three BAILIFFS stand amongst the tables. People eating lunch have all stopped to see what happens next. MRS BEGUM, RAHIM and ALI stand together.

> RUSSELL
>
> Ladies and gentlemen – lunch is over.

Some customers continue to eat.

> I said stop eating and put the fork down! Move!!

The customers quickly leave. RUSSELL is looking at his clipboard.

> Mrs Begum – do you have a licence to operate a restaurant from these premises?

> MRS BEGUM
> *(defiant)*
> We have always paid you on time.

> RUSSELL
> A licence, Mrs Begum – do you have one?

MRS BEGUM stares at RUSSELL.

> I'm closing you down. Gentlemen – health and safety.

The BAILIFFS put on goggles then erupt in an orgy of destruction. RAHIM sweeps his mother into the flat away from harm. With axes and sledgehammers they smash everything in sight – tables, chairs, flower pots. Then they move inside to continue their work.

INT: TUNNEL – AFTERNOON

The flickering silhouette of the LIGHTERLADY is seen far down the tunnel. Now she stops to open a heavy fire door in a recess. She passes through – EDDIE follows. Beyond the door is a much bigger tunnel – this is a passenger tunnel for a disused Underground station. The walls are tiled and there are old and peeling posters in display panels. Up ahead, the LIGHTERLADY's silhouette disappears down some stairs – the light goes with her.

INT: DISUSED UNDERGROUND STATION – AFTERNOON

We follow the LIGHTERLADY as she enters the cavernous black void of the platform.

A dull glow at the end of the platform grows in intensity. KEVIN walks through an arch onto the platform. He's in full boxing kit: shorts, boxer boots, satin robe – on the back of the robe is printed the legend 'I'LL DOUBLE IT NICKO'. He pulls back the hood as he approaches.

KEVIN

Did you see the cat?

LIGHTERLADY

What's that?

KEVIN

The cat's run off.

LIGHTERLADY
Oh, no, I didn't see it . . . You look pale.

EDDIE dips into a tunnel that runs parallel to the platform and quietly works his way down.

KEVIN (OOV)

Keeps the rats away . . .

KEVIN begins to unpack the rucksack – lots of tinned and ready-to-eat foods. He starts to eat a Scotch egg. He hasn't had a wash in a while – he has a two-week beard.

LIGHTERLADY (OOV)
You should shave . . .

EDDIE draws close to KEVIN and the LIGHTERLADY.

KEVIN

Did you phoned Nicko?

LIGHTERLADY *shakes her head.*

I asked you to phone him.

LIGHTERLADY

He's on holiday – he's away.

KEVIN

You still could've phoned. He might've come back early – he might be back here now 'cause he's – 'cause he's got food poisoning – see? – he might have food poisoning – salmonella, botulism, campylobacter, e-coli, legionnaire's . . . you don't know . . . not legionnaire's – wrong – fuck. (*shakes his head*)

LIGHTERLADY

You look pale.

KEVIN

Call him.

LIGHTERLADY

He's just a game show host – he can't help you.

KEVIN

Wrong – excuse me – he's a personal friend of mine.

KEVIN *munches and paces up and down the edge of the platform.*

Why you got to be so – if Nicko asks the question I know the answer. That's how it is . . . He asks the question, I know the answer.

The LIGHTERLADY *is gazing off into the gloom.*

LIGHTERLADY

Come back with me.

KEVIN

No.

LIGHTERLADY

I can't sleep at night – I keep thinking about what you done.

KEVIN

Mum – you don't – you don't know what it's like – it's different now – girls – it's like – look, I'm not going over this again – We've done this one – it's done – not again! (*pause*) What did you say to Linda?

LIGHTERLADY

Nothing.

KEVIN

Look at me.

LIGHTERLADY

Nothing.

KEVIN

That's good – good. Correct. Five points . . . Are you going to come tomorrow?

LIGHTERLADY

Come back with me, Kevin!

KEVIN

No! That's enough!

She looks crushed.

EXT: MRS PIERCE'S FLAT – AFTERNOON

RUSSELL *is knocking at the door – several other* BAILIFFS *stand close behind. Sound of Country & Western music.*

RUSSELL

Council inspection, open up. (*pause*) Knock it down.

RUSSELL *nods and three* BAILIFFS *charge the door with a battering ram.*

BAILIFF #1

Let me kick the fucker.

The door gives way. They all push through. MRS PIERCE *is wearing a cowboy outfit – she rushes the* BAILIFFS.

MRS PIERCE

You bloody arsehole bastards –

BAILIFF #1

Easy, tiger!

He sweeps her up and drags her back to the bedroom.

MRS PIERCE

You got no right – put me down – let me go! Let go of me you fucking –

An older client grabs his clothes and leaves. BAILIFF #1 throws MRS PIERCE on the bed – she's still shouting at the Bailiffs to get out. She makes a rush at RUSSELL – he slaps her face. MRS PIERCE staggers back and just as quickly rushes RUSSELL again.

BAILIFF #1

Shut the fuck up!

MRS PIERCE

You fucking arsehole!

MRS PIERCE has been pushed to the floor. She doesn't get up.

RUSSELL

Where's Eddie?

MRS PIERCE shakes her head with contempt.

MRS PIERCE

Oy yeah, I'm going to tell you – you stupid fucking dolt!

BAILIFF #2 has been searching the flat. He now enters.

BAILIFF #2

He ain't here.

RUSSELL

So . . . he's not here and you're not going to tell me where he is. I haven't got time for this.

Pause. RUSSELL gives his boys a slight nod.

Mrs Pierce – it's come to the Council's attention that you've been receiving swollen goods. Am I correct?

MRS PIERCE

Oh – you're a real caution, you are.

RUSSELL

Would you like a licence – a licence – would you like one, Mrs Pierce?

RUSSELL *crouches low and pushes his face menacingly close to* MRS PIERCE.

Would you like a licence?

INT: LINDA'S FLAT, FRONT ROOM – DAY

LINDA *is on top of* EDDIE *slapping and punching him – she is wild with rage -*

LINDA

Liar, liar liar! Shut up!

Both EDDIE *and* LINDA *are lying quietly on the floor breathing hard. After a few moments Linda gets up and heads out of the room.*

EDDIE

Linda?

LINDA

No.

EDDIE

Linda!

We hear the distant sound of retching.

INT: LINDA'S FLAT, FRONT ROOM – DAY

EDDIE *takes his jacket off and moves to the sofa. Almost immediately he falls asleep. Light streams in through the window and* EDDIE's *shadow sundials across the coffee table.*

INT: LINDA'S FLAT, FRONT ROOM – DAY

LINDA *walks in. She looks very ill.*

LINDA

Kill him.

LINDA *drops a package on* EDDIE's *lap.* EDDIE *awakes with a start. They stare at each other. Then* LINDA *walks out of the room. He takes a look in the package. There are several bundles of fifty pound notes.*

INT: LINDA'S FLAT, BEDROOM – DAY

EDDIE *knocks at Linda's bedroom door.*

EDDIE

Linda? Linda.

Suddenly there's a loud knocking at the front door. EDDIE *stuffs the packet of money inside his shirt and goes to answer. Looking through the spy-hole he sees* MOLLY *standing there. Another loud knock.*

Fuck it.

EDDIE *turns, walks smartly down the hallway and climbs out of a back window. We notice he's lost his shoes.*

EXT: SAXON – DAY

Before EDDIE *has made any distance he is brought face to face with* RAHIM.

RAHIM

You know where he is.

INT: BOILER ROOM – DAY

EDDIE *and* RAHIM *stand outside the small metal door that gives onto the inspection well.* RAHIM *is holding a torch and shaking with fear. He opens the door –* EDDIE *suddenly pushes it closed with a bang.*

EDDIE

No. Don't do this – here – here, it's yours.

EDDIE *pushes the packet of money at* RAHIM.

Now I'm paying you not to do this. There's a lot of money in here – you could get your family out of here – help your sister ... It's Kevin's money ...

Oh man . . . you don't get it, do you? You're small – you know
that, Eddie. Move out the way.

RAHIM *is furious – he pushes* EDDIE *out of the way.*

It's like this, yeah, Eddie –

RAHIM *whips out a knife and slashes his own arm.*

– it's like this, Eddie, yeah !

RAHIM *slashes himself again.*

– don't talk to me about money, all right?
RAHIM *has stopped shaking – he turns abruptly and passes through
the metal door – it slams shut.*

EXT: LANDING OUTSIDE MRS PIERCE'S FLAT – DAY

EDDIE *walks into shot – the flat is eerily quiet, but the fairy lights still
blink festively.* EDDIE *is about to knock but sees the door has been
smashed in. He enters.*

INT: MRS PIERCE'S FLAT – DAY

We follow EDDIE *as he walks through his mother's destroyed flat. In
the front room he finds his mother, sitting on the floor drinking vodka.
She is in a terrible state – her head has been shaved, she has a black
eye and blood on her face.*

EDDIE
Mum? Mum, it's me – it's Eddie.

He kneels down next to her.

MRS PIERCE
Eddie . . . Don't you worry about me Eddie – I'm fine . . . I'm
fine . . .

She turns away and drinks some more vodka. EDDIE *is crying.*

Have you eaten, Eddie? . . . ah come on, stop it it's nothing . . .
come on have a drink . . . have a drink Eddie.

EDDIE

It's not good for me, mum.

EDDIE *turns the bottle away.*

MRS PIERCE

Have a drink – have a drink with your old mum . . . me hair's
all gone . . .

MRS PIERCE *pushes the bottle back to* EDDIE . *He seems defeated.
He takes it and drinks from the neck – it doesn't go down easily.*

Good boy – good boy – you have a drink with your old mum.

EDDIE

Yeah.

INT: MRS PIERCE'S FLAT – DAY

We see EDDIE *staggering as he carries his mother to bed. We see him
cleaning her face with a cloth and water – they're both drunk.*

MRS PIERCE

You're a good boy, Eddie . . . my only lovely boy . . . go away –
get away from here . . . mmm? Best thing, Eddie – for me . . .

MRS PIERCE *drifts off to sleep.* EDDIE *is holding her hand. He lays his
head on the mattress and tries to rest her hand on his cheek.*

(*mumbling*)
What's that? Stop it – let me get some sleep, will you . . .

MRS PIERCE *turns over and goes to sleep again.*

EDDIE *goes back into the front room and looks again at the sprayed
graffiti on the wall – 'Serving You Right'.* EDDIE *takes a swig of vodka.*

EXT: SAXON – DAY

EDDIE *is walking across the estate. In the distance we see* MOLLY
pushing his handcart, his signature tune playing loudly. MOLLY *parks his
cart and walks towards* EDDIE *down the long empty concourse – this
looks like real cowboy stuff.* MOLLY *seems to be enjoying the moment.
As they get closer, he mimes drawing a gun and shooting* EDDIE.

MOLLY

Pow-pow!

EDDIE and MOLLY meet in the middle of the concourse.

Have you got something for me?

Mechanically EDDIE reaches for the packet of money inside his shirt.
Then he changes his mind and walks on past MOLLY.

Oy! – oy!

MOLLY walks after EDDIE – he makes kissing noises.

Hey, pussycat – if you want to play games . . . okay –

MOLLY grabs EDDIE's arm and tries to turn him.

I'm fucking talking to you!

EDDIE turns and strikes MOLLY down with a single hammer blow.
EDDIE walks on. MOLLY is having some kind of fit.

EXT: SAXON – DAY

EDDIE is walking towards the Bailiffs' Yard. As he draws closer, the big
double gates swing open and the Bailiffs' white van lurches out.
BAILIFF #1 is driving RUSSELL and BAILIFF #2 sit next to him. As

the van draws closer, EDDIE *pulls his shirt off and waves it in his hand
– he shouts at the top of his voice. He is half-naked, mad, and drunk.*

Unnoticed by EDDIE, *the envelope of cash has fallen to the ground.*
EDDIE *rushes the van – at the last minute the van breaks hard –*
EDDIE *jumps up on the bonnet and smashes the windscreen repeatedly
with his hammer. Then* EDDIE *bolts. The* BAILIFFS *jump out to give
chase but* EDDIE *is way ahead and dips out of sight.*

EXT: SAXON – DAY

The BAILIFFS *head back to the van.* BAILIFF #1 *sees the envelope
and picks it up.*

> RUSSELL
>
> Give it here.

RUSSELL *opens the envelope.*

> BAILIFF #1
>
> What is it, boss?

> RUSSELL
>
> None of your business.

RUSSELL *snatches another look in the envelope.*

EXT: SAXON – DAY

EDDIE *is slowing down – something's wrong.*

> EDDIE
> (*whispers*)
>
> Money . . .

EXT: SAXON – DAY

Here comes EDDIE *again – running back.* RUSSELL *watches as*
EDDIE *slows down and stops.*

> RUSSELL
>
> You want it – come and get it!

EDDIE *hesitates and then runs away again.*

EXT: SAXON – DAY

The LIGHTERLADY *sits alone with her galaxy of lighters. She is trying to spark up a lighter — it's obviously defective. She seems highly agitated. She shakes it vigorously.*

We see LINDA and the TWINS walking across the estate under an enormous black umbrella. They are all dressed in black; LINDA is wearing a low-cut dress and around her neck is a large gold crucifix — she looks like a grieving film star. A jumbo flies low overhead.

INT: DISUSED UNDERGROUND STATION – DAY

KEVIN *is shadow-boxing at the end of the platform in a small circle of light.*

                              KEVIN
... Mary, Bessie, James the Vain, Charlie, Charlie, James again. William and Mary, Anna –

KEVIN *has heard something. He looks off into the void and listens.*

   Mum?

KEVIN *picks up the torch and shines it down the platform.*

   Mum?

KEVIN *looks unsettled – he makes his way down the platform holding a torch in each hand – he plays the beams in all directions. Now he goes through an arch and enters the passenger tunnel between the platforms. A black cat darts out of the void and wraps himself around KEVIN's ankles. He crouches to stroke the cat. RAHIM glides up behind KEVIN and slits his throat.*

INT: JACKIE'S FLAT, FRONT ROOM – DAY

JACKIE *is listening to Flamenco music as she sweeps up drifts of hair. Now she opens the window and looks up as a plane climbs into the deep blue sky.*

EXT: SAXON – DAY (INT: LUTON VAN)

The three BAILIFFS *drive around the estate, looking for* EDDIE. *The windscreen has been punched out. Suddenly the driver starts spitting.*

                              RUSSELL
   What's the matter?

                             BAILIFF #1
   Sorry, boss – (*spit*) swallowed a fly (*spit*).

Horror: MOLLY, *masked in blood, staggers into the path of the van – smack – they run him down.*

RUSSELL

Stop!

BAILIFF #1

Jesus!

EXT: SAXON – DAY

EDDIE *is walking in a daze. Then a voice calls behind him:*

FRANKIE

Stop! I'm Mr Hoogewerff . . . Frankie Hoogewerff. You killed Barney!

FRANKIE *is wearing a sad saggy suit, and in his hands he carries a crossbow.* EDDIE *stops and turns.* FRANKIE *is scared and close to tears. He mumbles to himself.*

You killed my son . . .

EDDIE *remains motionless – an easy target.* FRANKIE *takes aim with his crossbow, fires and misses. He attempts to load again but his actions are clumsy and he drops the crossbow.*

No – wait. Jesus.

EDDIE *waits – he looks up at a plane climbing into the deep blue sky.* FRANKIE *loads and fires again.* EDDIE *staggers with the force of impact – the bolt has lodged in his thigh.*

EDDIE

Fuck.

EDDIE *sits down involuntarily.* FRANKIE *loads another bolt and takes aim and misses.* FRANKIE *is in tears – he walks up to* EDDIE *and throws all his bolts at him.*

FRANKIE

Look what you made me do – Jesus – what am I doing?! You killed my son! Jesus – you – you –

FRANKIE *raises the crossbow over his head and seems about to smash it down on* EDDIE's *skull. But* FRANKIE *goes slack and drops the crossbow. Emotionally drained, he walks away.*

103

EXT: SAXON – DAY

EDDIE *lies bleeding in the hot sun. There is no one around.*

EXT: SAXON – DAY

Here comes RUSSELL – *walking like doom towards* EDDIE.
He draws closer. EDDIE *sits up and faces him out. Now* RUSSELL *crouches next to* EDDIE.

RUSSELL
(nodding to crossbow)

You got a licence for that?

EDDIE

Russell – I'm going to kill you.

RUSSELL

Shhh – best not to talk . . .

RUSSELL *scans the estate.*

We better get you to hospital – fancy a lift in the van?

RUSSELL *gives the bolt a tweak –* EDDIE *screams with pain.*

That didn't hurt that much?

EDDIE

Fuck off.

RUSSELL *shakes the bolt –* EDDIE *screams again.*

JACKIE

Leave him alone.

JACKIE *is standing behind* RUSSELL *holding scissors.*

RUSSELL

'Hair by Jackie'. Nice. You better run home and lock the door . . .

JACKIE *doesn't move. He advances towards her.*

. . . 'cause here comes the wolf.

JACKIE *backs up.* RUSSELL *lunges and knocks the scissors out of her hand – he locks an arm around her neck and wrestles her to the ground.* RUSSELL *is on top of* JACKIE *now – he punches her in the face.* JACKIE *goes limp.*

... and you're going to get it –

Now EDDIE *is standing unsteadily behind* RUSSELL *holding the crossbow – he shoots a bolt into* RUSSELL's *head.* RUSSELL *turns and casts a surprised look at* EDDIE, *then sits back on his haunches. He continues staring, quite motionless. Suddenly he tries to get to his feet but lurches forward onto* JACKIE. *Dead. As a jet roars overhead,* JACKIE *wriggles out from under the bailiff's dead-ox weight. She lies on the ground shivering with shock and out of breath.* EDDIE *sits, and with one quick tug and cry of pain pulls out the bolt.*

EXT: SAXON – DAY

EDDIE and JACKIE stare at each other. They stare at RUSSELL. They stare at each other again.

EDDIE crawls over to RUSSELL and pulls the envelope of money out of his pocket. Another aeroplane roars overhead.

> EDDIE
>
> Jackie – I'm going to Spain – you coming?

> JACKIE
>
> What?

> EDDIE
>
> I said I'm going to Spain – you coming?

> JACKIE
>
> You're mad.

EDDIE wills her to come with his eyes.

> No!

EDDIE nods, turns and limps away. JACKIE looks around her – she has a sudden realisation.

> Stop – where are you going?!

EXT: SAXON – DAY

We see EDDIE limping along. A little way behind is JACKIE. They're making a slow getaway.

> JACKIE
>
> How much money have you got? Huh? I don't love you.
> Where's your shoes?

CAST AND CREDITS

Cast – in order of appearance

EDDIE	Sean Harris
FISHMONGERS	Tom Hopper, James Robinson, James Stokes
SALMON	Tony O'Leary
ALI	Ashley Sadanandan
RAHIM	Divian Ladwa
LINDA	Sarah Matravers
NICKO	Henry Kelly
CONTESTANTS	Michael Davidson, Kerry O'Halloran
KEVIN	Paul McNeilly
TWINS	Leigh and Jodie Woodward
LIGHTERLADY	Susan Scott
PEPPERSPRAY WOMAN	Maddie Loftin
BAILIFF #1	Luing Andrews
BAILIFF #2	Patrick MacRodain
SICK LADY	Jean Grover
BAILIFF #3	Jaime Goodbrand
JACKIE	Michelle Connolly
NADIMA	Farzana Dua Elahe
MRS BEGUM	Neelam Bakshi
MOLLY	Stephen Manwaring
SNOUT	Colin Campbell
FRANKIE HOOGEWERFF	David Mayberry
PISSHEAD	Charlie Hawkins
RUSSELL	Drew Edwards
TRAMP	Bunny Reed
GUN DEALER	Shammi Aulakh
DR FATIMA	Sandra Yaw
BROOM LADY	Jean Grover
MRS PIERCE	Sue Maund
MRS PIERCE'S CLIENT	Steve Mullins

Saxon Chorus
Matthew Brown, Mike 'X' Dixon, Snowden & Orphy Flood,
Jeanne Johnson, Christina Macklin, Sinead Macklin, Amy Minnette,
Michael Onder, Alan Petty, Nagini Rajendra, Annie Rhys,
Sajiv Sadanandan, Eric Sean Joni Sukumaran, Mark White

People of Saxon
Matthew Ackland, Gary Barnes, Robert Edward Barnes, C. Berry,
Louis Berry, Josie Beynes, Sebastian Billings, Ronald Norman
Botting, Angela Chance, Julia Chance, Nikki Cox, Julie Cutler,
Terry Giles, Aaron Gladwell, D. Gleeson, E. Gleeson, Reece Gorvin,
Karon Green, Kelly Green, Lucy Gurney, Natalie Gurney, Eamonn
Hennessy, Lydia Ilunga, Ricky Jordison, Bradley Knight, Valerie Ann
Malton, Lea Mazzocchi, Sylvia Mazzocchi, Darren Mouslou, Fey
Ogbuagu, Ajitha Sajeev, Charlie Vivian, Bianca Wells, Carli Wells,
Liam Wells, Warren Wells, Michaela Wilson

Production

DIRECTOR: Greg Loftin
PRODUCER: Elise Valmorbida
SCREENPLAY: Greg Loftin
LINE PRODUCER: Sam Parsons
DIRECTOR OF PHOTOGRAPHY: Steven Priovolos
MUSIC: Michael Portman and Vincent Browett

EXECUTIVE PRODUCERS: Elise Valmorbida, Greg Loftin,
   Jack Fidler, Barry Bassett

SCRIPT CONSULTANT: Elise Valmorbida
FIRST ASSISTANT DIRECTOR: Michael Studer
SECOND ASSISTANT DIRECTOR: Gene Keelan
THIRD ASSISTANT DIRECTOR: Cara Higgins
PRODUCTION COORDINATOR: Sebastian Billings
LOCATION MANAGER: Liz Cater
SCRIPT SUPERVISOR: Leigh Nicol

PRODUCTION DESIGNER: Jon Revell
ART/SET DRESSER: Rebecca Rainford
ART DEPARTMENT ASSISTANTS: Abi Jeary, Jaspreet Suraj
SET & PROP CONSTRUCTION: Henry Florence, Monica Corder

STUNT COORDINATORS: Tom Hyatt, Kevin McCurdy
FIGHT ARRANGER: Nicholas Hall

MAKE UP & HAIR DESIGNER: Sharon Holloway
PROSTHETICS: Sharon Holloway
MAKE UP & HAIR ARTIST: Jessica Davis
HAIR STYLIST: Beverly Chorlton

COSTUME DESIGNER: Andrew Joslin
ASSISTANT COSTUME DESIGNER: Vanessa Macdonald
WARDROBE ASSISTANTS: Laura Smith, Amy Ryan

FOCUS PULLER: Mihalis Margaritis
SECOND ASSISTANT CAMERA: Jaime Goodbrand
GAFFER: Michael Onder
BEST BOY: Paul Starkey
SPARK: Pawel Polak
ADDITIONAL SPARK: James Friend
CAMERA TRAINEE: Marvin McLeggan
STILLS PHOTOGRAPHERS: Steve Mullins, Elise Valmorbida

PRODUCTION SOUND MIXER: Simon Gillman
BOOM OPERATOR: Justin Smith

SENIOR RUNNER: Mike 'X' Dixon
RUNNERS: Darren Gian, Marvin McLeggan
ADDITIONAL RUNNERS: Michael Carr, Mark Jasper,
    Richard Leatherhead, John Prendergast

CASTING: Greg Loftin, Elise Valmorbida, Sam Parsons

CATERING: Gourmet Catering Ltd
CAMERA EQUIPMENT: VMI
LIGHTING: Lee Lighting
RADIOS: Audiolink
STOCK: Protape

WEBSITE: Michael Campbell
WEBSITE & AIRPORT GRAPHICS: word-design.co.uk

CORPORATE ACCOUNTANCY: Derek Rothera & Company
CORPORATE LAW: Bolt-Burdon
FILM/MEDIA LAW: Drew & Co

Post-Production

EDITOR: Greg Loftin
EDITING CONSULTANT: Richard Hughes
TITLES DESIGN: Steven Aspinall, Martin Shannon
DOUBLE OR QUITS GRAPHICS: Steven Aspinall, Martin Shannon

St Anne's Post:
HEAD OF PRODUCTION: Patrick Malone
ON-LINE EDITOR: Dan Preston
COLOURIST: Jamie Payne
RE-RECORDING MIXER: Mathew Knights
SUPERVISING SOUND EDITOR: Kevin Brazier
SOUND EDITORS: Anna Sulley, Louise Sinclair

Thanks

The residents of Roundshaw Estate, Wallington
The students and staff of Ravensbourne College of Design
   & Communication

Tom Abell	Siobhan Kelly
Tim Adler	Anita Lewton
Peter Barton	Kahloon Loke
Barry Bassett	Patrick Malone
Simon Campbell	Patrick McEnalley
David Castro	Matthew Miller
Kay Chudasama	Sally Ratcliffe
Andrew Curtis	Derek Rothera
Janet Evans	Michael Symons
Dennis Firminger	Thierry Swyndauw
Gloria Holloway	Camilla Tew
Mehran Imanzadeh	Dean Watkins
Mark Johnson	Barbara Wills
Mark Kebble	Pete York

Ascent Media Group, Aveda, Bolt-Burdon, Derek Rothera &
Company, Drew & Co, Hogarth Brown, R&B Taxi Repairs, Rajha
Shakiry, Reel Film Sutton, Rush Hairdresser's (Croydon), Simson's
Fisheries, The Windmill Pub (Wallington)

Special Thanks

Saxon was produced with the generous support of:

Jack 'Otto' Fidler

Lesley Gray

Matthew Brown

Jeanne Johnson
Suna Setna
Alma Valmorbida
Francesca Valmorbida McSteen

Susan Beaumont
Judy & Peter Morrissey
Steve Mullins
Alan Petty & Suzanne Goodband

Mary Bauer
Mirella Comparin
Charles Lunghinis
Nadia Valmorbida & Chris McSteen

Ross Alley
Sarah & Steven Aspinall
Vera Bettis
Rosi Braidotti & Anneke Smelik
Warren Coleman & Therese Kenyon
The Floods
James & Cleo Hamilton
Lily Kahan
Dena Kahan & Julian Silverman
Nagini & Raj Kajendra
Ann Latimer & Tony Hetherington
Audrey & Fred Loftin
Mark Loftin
Christina & Roger Thornton

Declan Buckley, Monique Dorigo & Arthur Aroney,
Penny & John Madden, John McGrath, Tim Richards

Music

'Cielito Lindo'
Composition: traditional
Arrangement: Michael Portman and Vincent Browett
Vocalist: Eddine Saïd

'Molly Malone'
Composition: traditional
Arrangement: Michael Portman and Vincent Browett

'Drifting'
Composition: Michael Portman and Vincent Browett
Vocalist: Michael Portman

'Someone to Love You'
Composition: Michael Portman and Vincent Browett
Arrangement: Michael Portman and Vincent Browett
Vocalists: Michael Portman

'Cielito Punk' ('Cielito Lindo')
Composition: traditional
Arrangement: Michael Portman and Vincent Browett
Vocalists: Michael Portman and Vincent Browett

Additional guitars: Rolph Angelucci-Edwards
Additional drums: Sean Heaphy
Mexican trumpet: Siân Allen

Original score composed, arranged, performed and recorded by
Michael Portman and Vincent Browett

Filmed on location at the Roundshaw Estate, Wallington,
near Croydon, UK

SEAN HARRIS – lead actor

SEAN HARRIS memorably played Joy Division's Ian Curtis in
24-Hour Party People. After co-starring in *Asylum* (by *Young
Adam* director David Mackenzie, with Ian McKellen and Natasha
Richardson) and *Creep*, Sean played 'Mr Big' Nick Sidney in
Brothers of the Head, causing a stir at the Toronto, Berlin and
Edinburgh Film Festivals of 2006. He played Moors murderer Ian
Brady in the acclaimed Granada two-part drama *See No Evil*,
broadcast to millions of viewers in the UK and winner of the
BAFTA Award for Best Television Drama 2007. Sean is the fat man
who gets very thin in Mark Ronson's cult pop promo.

'Just as Clint Eastwood was the Man With No Name, Harris tends
to be the Actor With No Name. The face is familiar, and when you
see it appear in a film it's a guarantee of a notable performance to
come. Yet so completely does he tend to disappear into a character . . .
Saxon is his chance to make an impression and he falls on it like a
starving man spying a plate of pork chops.'
– Alison Rowat, *The Herald*

ABOUT THE DIRECTOR AND PRODUCER

Writer-director GREG LOFTIN's debut feature film *Saxon* follows
years of rigorous script development. He runs his own production
company, writing original scripts and directing short films. Greg
works at Ravensbourne College of Communication, where he leads
the Foundation Degree in Broadcast Post-Production. His eagerly
awaited second feature screenplay *The Hand Factory* is currently
in development.

Producer ELISE VALMORBIDA worked with Greg Loftin on the
script, casting and funding of *Saxon*. In 2007 she was awarded the
honour of Trailblazer by Skillset and the Edinburgh International
Film Festival. *Saxon* is her first feature. Elise has worked for many
years as creative director with leading international brands. She is
a published writer and a member of 26 and NPA.